T0007451

THE WITCH OF EYE

KATHRYN NUERNBERGER

ESSAYS

 SARABANDE BOOKS Louisville, KY

THE
WITCH
OF
EYE

Library of Congress Cataloging-in-Publication Data

Names: Nuernberger, Kathryn, author.
Title: The witch of eye : essays / Kathryn Nuernberger.
Description: Louisville, KY : Sarabande Books, 2021
Identifiers: LCCN 2020016771 (print) | LCCN 2020016772 (e-book)
ISBN 9781946448705 (paperback) | ISBN 9781946448712 (e-book)
Subjects: LCSH: Witches—Biography. | Women—Miscellanea.
Marginality, Social. | Witchcraft—History.
Classification: LCC BF1571.5.W66 N84 201 (print)
LCC BF1571.5.W66 (e-book) | DDC 133.4/30922 [B]—dc23
LC record available at https://lccn.loc.gov/2020016771
LC e-book record available at https://lccn.loc.gov/2020016772

Cover and interior design by Alban Fischer.
Printed in Canada.
This book is printed on acid-free paper.
Sarabande Books is a nonprofit literary organization.

This project is supported in part by an award from the National
Endowment for the Arts. The Kentucky Arts Council, the state
arts agency, supports Sarabande Books with state tax dollars and
federal funding from the National Endowment for the Arts.

for M. Patricia Nuernberger, PhD,
my mother

&

Sam Nuernberger,
my sister

Contents

THE WITCH OF EYE

Hag, Crone, Cunning Woman, Witch

An aspen grove lives for a thousand years, the tongues of the leaves shaking after the wind. No aspen tree is just a tree, each is also a limb rooted into a much larger body that is an entire forest breathing together.

They called the old women crones, hags, cunning women, and witches. Names to make a daughter think she should devote herself to becoming something, anything, other than what she is. Like the women I descend from, the ones called hysterics and manics, obsessives and depressives, I feel as if I have an aspen grove that stretches from my stomach to my throat. Sometimes I can hardly speak for trying to hush those leaves.

This little apothecary I keep of wild lettuce, St. John's wort, a dozen jars of elderberry syrup, is a way of saying to myself what I need to know of myself. My great-grandmother swore by Lydia Pinkham's compound of unicorn root, life root, black cohosh, pleurisy root, and fenugreek seed preserved in 19 percent alcohol, so I keep a half-empty bottle dug from a barn loft fifty years ago on the shelf. My grandmother, locked away by a patriarchy of doctors who didn't want to ask and didn't want to know, never stopped calling for someone to bring the pills, so I keep an unopened cardboard tube labeled Lithium Carbonate and stamped 1968 there too. I keep an even older medicine I found among the forced confessions and brutal executions, a torn page with a little spell to cure your ague, that ancient disease of trembling.

It was no cure, how I begged God to turn me into a bear or a cow, a constellation, or winter. No use translating myself into lullabies or ending every sentence with "I'm sorry." For no use I ran like a woman wishing to be released into the still silence of a laurel tree.

The aspen leaves shake because the cross was made of aspen wood. Or, the leaves shake because this is where the wives gather to tremble their tongues. Or, the leaves shake because the tree was cursed by Jesus after it would not acknowledge him when he spoke to it. This was after he smote a fig tree just because it was winter and the tree could bear no fruit for him. There are so many stories in the margins about what an asshole that young, handsome Jesus could be.

For a thousand years the theory of medicine was the same as the theory of magic. Called the Doctrine of Signatures, the axiom was that herbs resemble the parts of the body that they can be used to treat. Toothwort has those baby teeth blossoms; eyebright blinks its petals. Walnuts have the perfect signature of your aching head. The theory is that the world is talking to us. The theory is that God is talking to us through the world.

William Henderson did not save the name of the woman who gave him the spell I have come to think of as "Spell for the Likes of Me" to be included in his Notes on the Folk-Lore of the Northern Counties of England and the Borders. If he even asked her about it, he made no notes of what it had taken for her to carry such knowledge into a future one hundred years beyond the last witch trial.

I cut a lock of my hair and used it to bind the bark, wishing, I thought, to be turned into the kind of woman who can hold still and keep her peace. Whether or not it worked is a complicated question tied to the larger question of whether or not I wanted it to. There were words to go along with that ribbon of hair laid against the wood and I hesitated to say them. What is it to live, I wonder, if not to tremble?

Not only did the aspen tree refuse to bow before the Lord, but it declared that it was free of sin and had no reason to weep. This is the tree, the clerics say, that became the cross. This is the tree used to pierce the buried body of a witch through the heart to prevent her from rising again.

Watching my lock sway in the wind, I thought about the elixirs and unguents, the scoldings and catechisms I have been offered as a way of living into some shape and form and voice twisted away from my own. The Doctrine of Signatures promises God created "Herbes for the use of men, and hath given them particular Signatures, whereby a man may read . . . the use of them." It promises you can find a resemblance of yourself that will be your medicine somewhere in these woods.

Among those old bowers it felt then as if a metaphor of myself separated back into its two halves—there was me and there was the woman I have been afraid of becoming looking back. The vision perhaps was magic or perhaps it is just what the words do if you let yourself say them. "Aspen tree, aspen tree," the old spell goes, "I prithee, shiver and shake instead of me."

A day may come, if I live this life as well and courageously as I hope I can, when a tribunal decides to stake a branch into my old heart to hold me down. As if it weren't rooted there already. I will not bow down just because some man who withered a fig is passing by. I am going to spill every last leaf into the ear of this endless wind.

Lisbet Nypan

—FOR LYN COOPER (1951–2013)

The settlement of Lisbet Nypan's estate was assessed at eighty-five silver coins—quite a comfortable living for a wife and a tenant farmer. Their wealth came from Lisbet's practice of healing muscle aches and rheumatism by conducting rituals of salt.

When questioned, she was only too glad to explain her methods. This, after all, was her business and had been for over forty successful years.

She would lay salts over the body of the afflicted and smooth them with massaging hands as she prayed:

> Jesus rode over the moors, he stood forth
> and made the leg, Lord in flesh, skin, bones
> ever since as before. God's word. Amen.

Then she brushed all that salt onto a plate and either she ate the salt or the patient did. One woman testified that Lisbet cured her pains and agony by giving her a potion of soil, water, and salt. She said this not with malice but gratitude. And confusion. Had Lisbet sinned? Had she? It had never occurred to her that this could be wrong.

Lisbet's husband was prideful and short-tempered. Also, he was an idiot. In disputes with neighbors he would raise his gnarled, seventy-year-old finger and scold, "You forget who my wife is." I like him for the way he seems to have thought of himself as belonging to her as much as she belonged to him. For the way he was proud of her. He must have been very sorry about all that foolish pride, though, when he had to watch her die before they cut off his head.

During the trial, he followed Lisbet's lead and refused to confess to witchcraft or to admit wrongdoing in any way. Perhaps their three children, grown, with children of their own, wished their parents would say what the prosecutors wanted to hear. But to Lisbet these inquisitors were nothing more than boys, that eager generation of sons the people sent south to University so they would have an "educated" clergy. The boys came home from Belgium and Germany and environs as young men now and obsessed with the spectral evidence and inquisition that were so popular in the churches of the lowlands. She would never plead to such as these, and certainly she would never apologize for herself.

I too have known some very good and steadfast women. You could not make them say words they did not want to say. Nor could you make them sorry.

But they didn't start that way either. They are the first to tell you many of us start out meek, as beautiful virtuous apologies of ourselves until, if we let them, the passing years make some more meaningful purpose of our lives.

One of these women Lisbet Nypan reminds me of is Lyn Cooper, who was sometimes like an aunt to me, sometimes like a friend. She'd been a nun and she'd been an ex-nun, in the closet and out of it, so she knew a little bit of almost anything a person might feel. If you visited her house, she'd put you to work, drinking and stuffing envelopes for the next fundraiser. If you had AIDS in those terrible early years and your family wouldn't know you, even if you were dying; if doctors were afraid to touch you, even if you were dying; if anyone who knew of what you were dying might turn away, you went to Lyn, who built one hospice in our city after another. If you were being abused or your children were, you went to Lyn's partner, Maggie, who built one safe house after another. If you were thinking about giving up on some difficult thing you had set out to do, you went to Lyn and she told you to get it together and you believed her that you would.

Once, on a business trip to a very nice golf course with developers and financers, she slipped her favorite, most cheerful of blowhards a pot brownie. He didn't notice the difference, but talked longer and faster about urban development until she was so bored driving the highway of his visions that she told him he was stoned and to shut up already.

To pull such a prank and be loved even more for it, you would have to be some kind of witch. When another of the men flew into one of his characteristic rages, throwing his putter across the green and storming off to kick at the sand trap, she asked him over a beer later why he was really so angry. Chewing a cigar on the balcony of her wake, he would say the simplicity of that question opened up the rest of his life. He was not the same person he had once been.

This is a very old world. You could spend your whole century just trying to count its revolutions. Elijah threw salt in the water at Jericho. David struck down eighteen thousand Edomites in the Valley of Salt. In the first century of Christianity the converted savored the blessed salts as well as the dunk of baptismal waters. Saint Augustine of Hippo called savoring the salts one of the visible forms of grace. John the Deacon explained the use of salt in this way: "So the mind, drenched and weakened by the waves of this world, is held steady."

When Jesus ached, his own mother treated him with the ritual of reading over the salts. Lisbet Nypan told this to the court, not as a confession—she would never give them a "right" confession— but as an explanation for those who seemed to know so little about where pain comes from and where it might go.

Walpurga Hausmännin

The herein mentioned, malefic and miserable woman, Walpurga Hausmännin, now imprisoned and in chains has, upon kindly questioning and torture, following on persistent and fully justified accusations, confessed her witchcraft." Or so says the "Judgement on the Witch Walpurga Hausmännin," a court record translated by E. William Monter in *European Witchcraft*.

The second child of Anna Kromt, the one Magdalena Seilerin delivered prematurely, a child of Stoffel Schmidt—two pages of accounts, forty-one in all. Walpurga killed, she said at her trial, by rubbing salve on the children or putting something in the mother's drink or rubbing salve on the mother's belly.

Also with her ointment she brought about the deaths of Leinhart Geilen's three cows, Max Petzel's cow, Duri Striegl's cow, Hans Striegl's cow, a cow of the governor's wife, a cow of Frau Schötterin, a cow of Michael Kilnger, and Bruchbauer's horse.

She said she dug up the bones of children to make hail over the county on two separate occasions. "She confesses likewise, that the blood she sucked from the child, she had to spit out again before the devil, as he had need of it to concoct a salve."

Reading the court reporter's summary of her confessions, one wonders which parts the woman believed were true. For example, when "the above-mentioned Walpurga confesses that she oft and much rode on a pitchfork at night with her paramour," was she just saying anything to get that hot poker off her back or had she once stumbled into the woods tripping medieval magic mushroom balls?

The way the story of the court records goes, when she was newly widowed, Walpurga cut corn for Hans Schlumperger. In that field she made arrangements for sex with Bis im Pfarrhof. "Him she enticed with lewd speeches and gestures." But instead, at the agreed-upon hour, a demon named Federlin came to her in this man's clothes. After fornication she felt the cloven hoof of the whoremonger, who promised to save her from her poverty. She flew with him sometimes on a pitchfork.

For thirty years she worked as a licensed midwife, which meant induced labor, pain meds, birth control, fertility treatments, and abortion. It meant woman who gives you choices you didn't think you were allowed to have. It meant woman who knows more of death and birth than anyone else in a village in a century when everyone knew so much of both.

It's hard to resist the sense that you can hear truth inside the confessions. Far more likely you've just caught an echo of something about yourself. For example, I think Walpurga had feelings for that corn-cutter who turned out to be something else altogether. I think for a time she felt wanton and reckless and happy. And that she was sorry about it later.

She was wrong of course to feel guilty. Our lives are so short as it is. But hers was a different sort of time and anyway what is right and wrong to a feeling?

After they tortured and burned her, they dumped her ashes in the nearest flowing stream. This last part at least seems right to me. After absorbing every crime the village had ever known, every stillbirth, every miscarriage, every sick cow, so the inquisition of Dillingen, Germany, could be snuffed out with her, she ought to be have been set free to wander the aimless drift of water down through one forest and field after another.

She says she is sorry so many times in these records. She seems to really believe she deserves what is happening to her. Centuries later, I want to absolve her of this cruel spell the judges put on her. To say, "Walpurga, who among us?"

To add that it was only when I came to the end of my capacity for so much pointless guilt that I understood deeper than that sorry fear was need. Need of something to float on that was not just another abyss. Need of an old forest growing wild in defiance of all reason. Need of an unreal world beyond all this.

It is the midwife who understands when we are giving birth to someone we are learning the history of dying — the lover, if they are not in some other room pretending there is nothing they don't already know, watching all that blood pour from this person giving birth; this person giving birth watching the lights in the room dim to one polestar of pain; this third person to say something that sounds like "baby," to catch something in her hands she says is your baby. I was not alone in the room, but it felt as if I was learning all of it alone.

I have needed Walpurga Hausmännin to explain how you can come back from this. Here in this chaos of honeysuckle and wild grape vines with stems as thick as your arms clamoring the pines, among those invisible calls of owls and nightjars, the quivering constellations of fireflies trying to find each other, the water makes such a nice song of itself as it passes by. Walpurga, who has learned how to be here and how to be here without being here.

Agnes Waterhouse

Agnes Waterhouse, age sixty-four in the year 1566, was an impoverished woman who had a white cat named Sathan that spoke in a strange, hollow voice and would do anything for a drop of blood. She had him kill her pig to prove what he could do, and then had him kill the cows and geese of her neighbors, with whom she had quarreled; neighbors themselves, with whom she had quarreled; her husband, with whom she had quarreled.

Government officials tortured her, of course, to wring out this weird confession, but they wouldn't necessarily have had to. There is ample research to suggest that a little menace, a little kindness, the promise of approval from someone in authority—this is enough, even today, to make people very confused about what they know to be true.

Her daughter Joan, for instance, was induced to confess she had seen her mother turn that cat into a toad. Why turn your demon cat into a demon toad? You might as well ask why a police officer would kill a man for selling cigarettes or taking out his wallet or carrying a cell phone, living in his apartment, or opening his own front door. The child went on to admit she sold her own soul to that selfsame toad so she could get a bit of bread and cheese from the neighbor girl, Agnes Brown.

Of course the tribunal believed this testimony. People *knew* the devil to be real, and his magic, his witches, his familiars, his blood spells and poison. Their whole lives they knew the devil was coming for them. This century is not so different. Consider the mug shot and some blurry footage from a gas station calling into being that archetype of white America's inquisitions. The officer will say in the deposition that he was "like some sort of superhuman beast bulking up to run through the shots." That's the only way such tribunals can imagine a now-dead Black teenager. "Like a demon." The mostly white jurors will nod like people who know, and then they will acquit.

In a witch hunt, a great many of the witches confess. Why would they do that if they weren't guilty? Well, here's part of a reason why: The Supreme Court ruled in *Frazier v. Cupp* that the police may willingly and knowingly use deception in the course of interviewing a suspect, even though misinformation renders people vulnerable to manipulation. Michel Foucault, the great philosopher of discipline and punishment, reminds us the confessional process is always guided by rules that "are necessarily of the master's side, rules that once again do not focus on the truth of discourse, but on the way in which this discourse of truth is formulated." Among individuals exonerated after wrongful conviction, researchers found that 85 percent of juvenile false confessions were given by Black children. Contrary to certain popular narratives about power and control, the earliest forms of law enforcement were not well-regulated militias, but slave patrols hunting down people running for freedom. A 2006 FBI bulletin detailed the threat and warned the consequences of white supremacists infiltrating local and state law enforcement would be more excessive uses of force, more extrajudicial killings, less successful prosecution of hate crimes.

So the neighbor girl wasn't surprised when little Joan Waterhouse brought over her mother's demon familiar to scare her in some new horrific form. She was frightened, of course, by the contorted face and horns she thought she saw, the violence of the voice when he demanded she give him butter. But also she'd been expecting this would happen ever since everyone started telling her it would.

It seems to be easier for some people to understand the role of stereotype threat and implicit bias in the judicial system when I say the wrongful imprisonment and execution happened to a little old white lady, gullible and confused, possibly suffering from dementia, named Agnes. As she stood at the gallows awaiting the rope, Agnes Waterhouse pleaded with the authorities, Reverend Thomas Cole, Sir John Fortescue, Sir Gilbert Gerard, the Queen's attorney, and John Southcote, Justice of the Queen's Bench. She begged their forgiveness and the forgiveness of God. She swore she'd never stopped praying, but only used Latin because that wretched cat forbade her to pray in English. She swore before the mob of people that even when she'd been stripped by the devil of her right to speak, as the devil might do to any of them, still she'd kept trying, she'd never stopped trying, to find a way to live honorably within this system of God's laws and men's.

The Invention of Fire

Less monotonous and less abstract than flowing water, even more
quick to grow and to change than the young bird we watch every day
in its nest in the bushes, fire suggests the desire to change, to speed
up the passage of time, to bring all of life to its conclusions.

— GASTON BACHELARD, *The Psychoanalysis of Fire*

I n "Burning of Three Witches in Baden, Switzerland," dated
to 1585, three women lie on a large pyre watched by a circle
of men. The smoke forms a silhouette of inquisitors with
their hoods up, lurking at the periphery of the crowd. The flames
are unexpectedly hard-edged and geometrical, each lick stabbing
the next in acute angles.

———

You can find many images of what was done to witches in the
scrapbook of the Protestant minister Johann Jakob Wick. He called
it his *Wickiana* and in it compiled news documents from 1505 to
1588, presumably as evidence of a coming apocalypse. Among

depictions of grasshoppers, comets, and children attacked by pigs were many images of the executions of witches. These in addition to the oil paintings in museums and miniatures lining the margins of illuminated manuscripts. Each one I see reminds me how deeply I agree with Susan Sontag's objections to the propagation of images of war, outlined in *Regarding the Pain of Others*. Maybe the images' effect will be to trigger apathetics' empathy and stop the violence, but more likely they will galvanize the rage of the faithful and teach the ambitious more of what a human being is capable.

I am neither lying nor exaggerating—in "The Torture Used against Witches" (1577) the cherubic boy-man with curly locks has a boner so big it almost interferes with his capacity to turn the wheel that pulls the woman's arms unaccountably backwards, rendering the deep green of her dress very striking against the crimson of her apron. The parchment is centuries old and tattered, but the pigments have not lost a shade. Or maybe someone came back later to add this color so they could imagine the moment more vividly.

It is harder than we think to imagine someone else's pain. Elaine Scarry explains this in her treatise on suffering, *The Body in Pain: The Making and Unmaking of the World*. It is even a struggle to clearly remember our own agony after it is over, much less someone else's. Psychologists theorize that those who torture suffer from an isolating sickness of not being able to derive a sense of others' emotions from cues of facial expression, body language, and tone of voice. This is not to say their suffering is equivalent to that of those they tortured. Only to help us consider the extremes a person might go to for the relief of seeing some other person's humanity. We suffer from each other and we suffer without each other.

In the British Library's MS Royal 20 C VII, f. 4v there is pity in the woodcut eyes of the people watching; the bridled horses they sit astride have only the most merciless gaze. I am reminded of this tip for interpreting dreams: every character is a different version of yourself.

Turn the page if you can stand to look into the face of the man amidst those first tentative licks the pitchfork peasant tends and you'll see he is weeping, but softly, as any of us knows how to weep.

———

Walpurga Hausmännin suffered one of the very worst executions I know of. For a long time I didn't write it—my memory of the Museum of Torture is still fresh. The instruments were as real as that stag party of drunk bachelors ahead of me, laughing as they passed scold's bridles, lead shoes, collections of variously sized wheels. They hung on each other's shoulders while singing a loud and slurring bar song about the wanton maid who roasted six pears but only gave her betrothed two.

———————

This executioner in a *Wickiana* entry from 1587 is like a dancer with his massive thighs and slender knees, a delicate right foot *en pointe* as he reaches for a stick of wood with a flourish of the right arm. The waifs at the stake are wailing, but their faces are charcoal-smudged so it is easier to keep looking.

Pain is private and there is no easy way to put it on display that does not have a titillating quality. Though it is the case that making someone look is sometimes used as a form of torture and is sometimes used in the making and training of torturers, nevertheless, there is something to be said for recounting the truth of what was done and also for opening yourself up to the pain of knowing it.

———————

Walpurga Hausmännin was stopped five times before she reached the town square. First they tore her left breast and right arm with irons. Then they tore her right breast. At the third stop they tore her left arm. At the fourth her left hand was cut off. They paused at the stake to cut off her right hand before lighting the fire.

The medieval Europeans were such an allegorical people. Nothing meant what it was. Walpurga's torture is unbearable in all of its meanings. The left hand was cut because "if mine eye offend me." The right hand because it was the one she used to take her oath as a midwife. Her breasts and arms were torn because it was believed the devil took away almost all of a witch's capacity to feel. And the fire because "none shall suffer a witch to live" and "their portion will be in the lake that burns with fire." In general, the faces of the women in the flames will be unlikely in the allegorical extreme—peaceful or penitent or snarling as a demon would. Hans-Jurgen Gunther showed a red-winged dragon with sagging breasts and the face of a pig pulling something ephemeral (a soul? a demon? her raspy and cracking voice?) out of a woman burning alive with her hands tied behind her back. To convey her face of pain would be beside the point—an execution is not about the pain of the dying, it is about the symbols those who are compelled to watch can't help but interpret.

In the *Spiezer Chronik* (1485) Jan Hus sits with a flame of yellow hair inside a blossom of fire, smiling. He looks like the illustration in my daughter's picture book of Thumbelina just born from a peony. The man poking him with a pitchfork wears the expression of dismay.

If you must look, interpret instead the quizzical faces of those who are trying to figure out what this sign is telling them. Or how they wear the open-mouthed astonishment of someone who just figured out what it all means.

———

Medieval European art marches through the centuries on a trajectory from profoundly and awkwardly two-dimensional toward an ever-more-realistic illusion of depth and perception that would be perfected in the Age of Enlightenment, when witch trials became an embarrassing old superstition while the torments of slavery emerged as the backbone of modern economies. But in some cases the depiction of flames skipped over all that slow evolution, with a viewfinder straight into the minds of the postwar abstract expressionists melting the paint of their feelings like the center of an atom bomb.

The abstraction of fire is a constant through the centuries, including in the work of J. M. W. Turner, who painted sea battles and Parliament on fire because a burning sky is permission to brush on the chaos of what you see beyond seeing as your hand trembles its work beyond reason. Whistler was another of these apostles of flames, painting a series of nocturnes, in which the night is so many layers of abstracted shades of darkness and the fireworks fall in a formless but beautiful drizzle of gold leafing.

On occasion one of these anonymous painters working on this or that chronicle in the solitude of the monastery looks away from the face they cannot show to the fire itself. If you set a person on fire, the horror of such abstractions show, eventually their face stops being a face and becomes part of the fire. In the movies they can only make this look campy and implausible. But on the canvas it is painful and teaches you how to feel. Hard to look and hard to look away, they are images that make you want to undo time. The power in such radical allegories is that they simplify what is and what it means to the same breath: Everyone is as fragile as you are.

Two Elizabeths

From each witch they interrogated the inquisitors needed something old—a Sabbath orgy or blood oath or cat demon or wolf-faced baby or some other verification of the stories they already believed. But they also needed something new, so they could feel with each trial and execution as if they were making progress.

Elizabeth Styles's addition to the canon: She let her demon suck her blood. He came to her often. Even when she was tied to a pole in a dungeon, still he came to her in the form of a butterfly to suck from her as he always did.

Though it may seem strange to us now, that the devil came as an apparition of a butterfly was not something new then. Even the great botanist and first ecologist, Maria Sibylla Merian, who discovered and documented insect metamorphosis in the 1600s, had to be careful about her reputation, because there were many who still believed in witches and their power to take the form of butterflies and spoil the milk. She kept her laboratory of silkworms and caterpillars very secret.

The Greeks, who had a rich tradition of witchcraft, called butterflies psyches, the same word they used for souls. I wonder about that, about what in each of us is a little bit witch. In his book *Psyche*, Jacques Derrida writes about how each moment of speech, each endeavor to charm or interest a listener, is an invention. An invention, he says, is by its nature an attempt to unsettle the status quo. It requires a moment of destruction. He writes, "An invention always presupposes some illegality, the breaking of an implicit contract." And adds, "A strange proposition. We have said that every invention tends to unsettle the statutes that one would like to assign it at the moment it takes place." The butterfly of us then, the witch of us, is our striving to be something to each other.

Elizabeth Styles was accused by a thirteen-year-old girl also named Elizabeth. This other Elizabeth had been having strange fits lasting three hours or more and when the episode had passed she'd have holes in her hands, wrists, face, and neck. There would be thorns in her flesh. For this she blamed Elizabeth.

In addition to the butterfly business, Styles confessed that the devil had appeared to her about ten years since in the form of a handsome man or sometimes a black dog who promised her money, she said, and that she should live gallantly and have "The Pleasure of the World" for twelve years if she would blood-sign his paper, handing over her soul to him.

In his chapter on witchcraft theory, the historian Walter Stephens suggests inquisitors were conducting a form of theological research in their trials. They were anticipating the invention of empirical data and a scientific method, after a fashion, and so were inventing the proof they were desperate to receive.

"The attitude of witchcraft theorists toward their theories was not belief," Stephens writes, "but rather resistance to skepticism, a desperate attempt to maintain belief, and it betrays an uncommonly desperate need to believe." We could say, then, that Elizabeth Styles's inquisitor was one of the great innovators in his time.

What a comfort it would be if we could believe criminal justice as literary genre was a phenomenon of the past. If it was only once upon a time that interrogations were a form of coauthorship between the accuser and the accused.

Psyche is the part of you that can be separated from your body. This capacity to become yourself and your other self creates opportunities for feelings like romance and ecstasy. And if you are someone who can't seem to get yourself free of yourself? Well, perhaps you will be consoled by watching others escape the self of their bodies. Torture gets the soul out almost every time.

To have a soul then is to flutter about spoiling the milk and destabilizing the script of how we talk to each other.

I often feel like a witch in the way I do a poor job performing the part of a friend or friendly or casual acquaintance. This is because I want to charm, to show kindness, to understand, to console, to be someone to the people I meet, and the script only allows us to pass each other briefly and superficially without creating an event. I always love an event. Therefore, if need be, I will be the event that happened to you. Like a kindness.

Say for example you're a soldier walking home from the war. Or the maiden working in your stepmother's garden. Or the miller with a cart and a broken axle. A wild-haired woman will stop and, in her kindness, give you a gift of great power and significance. A jewelry box, for example, that can summon three dogs of great, greater, and greatest size. Or a letter from that old love you try never to think of. Maybe a bag that can hold everything up to and including death itself. And now your ordinary life of meandering pleasures is jacked up with purpose and an unwieldy power that may be a help to you but may also rear its head back and bite you a curse on your nose.

I used to take vows of silence every morning because of how my love and fear of invention could make me so sick to my stomach. In this way conversational invention is like any other endeavor at which you might fail.

When I hiked up a mountain with an old dear friend, I was so excited because I have a good, amusing script for mountains I invented back when I lived near one and went up it every Saturday. It involves cursing and hating the mountain all the way up because when the path is just sharp stones pointing ever higher you can tell the mountain is trying to push you down. But then you finally reach the lake and you and the crags can admit to each other that you were actually in love this whole time.

What I've always loved about this friend of mine is how easy he is to charm and how he is full of unexpected questions that inspire you to inventions. His admiration for an unexpected comment lights up the room. But there have been a few intervening years between us and I didn't know he'd been busy all this time turning into a man who conquers peaks at such a breakneck pace you can't keep up to talk to him. On the mountain, charm is not what's on his mind.

I know it is an absurd exaggeration, but there are days when I feel like the rag woman with cobwebs in my hair muttering a shuffle at the edge of town. I'm the kind of witch that means well, but I know when someone is so invented, so off, it's hard for someone else to say whether they mean well or not and even if they do mean well, whether they are capable of doing well with all that meaning.

When I see the woodcuts of these hand-tied women waiting for their stick of flame, I wonder why they couldn't just keep it to themselves. Is it really so hard to pretend?

And that's the reason I like these failed witches so much. It feels hard to me to resist invention because it really is. Like a moth to the flame, so many of us seek after the inventions that disturb the norms, the statutes, or the rules. I want to be kind, want to make something of that kindness, but I am an inventor and this mind can't stop inventing, though this mouth has no mind of its own to run it more smoothly along the track of the social contract it also has no hand to sign and no will to.

There are aspects of an inquisition I would probably enjoy. The collaborative invention of the world we might all wish were true would be one part. Adding decorative touches to the archetype of the devil would be another. It's the kind of game my friend and I used to play every Monday at the bar. What are the names of the horses pulling your personal chariot of the apocalypse? What's in your sack of fascist tropes tonight? What three embellishments would you devise when your turn came to host the witches' Sabbath?

On the mountain most of my words were answered with silence, but when I was gasping and holding my side, he offered this: "To get fast, you have to realize you aren't going to drown. There's air everywhere out here, so let the breathing take care of itself." And on the way down when I was crab-crawling my way through the slipping dust he said, between a hop and a stride, "Try it like a drunken monk."

Driving home I excoriated myself for my so-much dumb joking about that bitch of a mountain. I had been with my friend, but I still missed him. After years and much else, your friend may be the same river, but he is not the same water. And now all of my memories were the grating sound of my own stuck gears.

The vow of silence is not necessarily a refusal to invent. It is not necessarily a retreat into yourself. It can simply be a promise not to invent each other. On a surprising note of hope for the future of human relationships, given that he is the philosopher who proved over and again how we cannot say what we mean, Derrida concludes, "The other is what is never inventable and will never have waited for your invention."

Not so long ago at a family brunch I remarked that our gregarious father had tried so hard to teach me how to get along with other people. When I was a timid and awkward girl, he tried to make it seem so simple—just ask them questions about themselves and their interests, he said. People love to talk about themselves and they will feel you are being kind. I remarked that after twenty years of practice, I think I might be getting good at it.

My brother, who is mostly a silent person but skillful at the "sports team" and "home remodeling" scripts, chuckled when he said, "Yeah, but your questions are all like"—and here he switched on his best head-cocked robot voice—"'How does it feel to be you, Human?'"

Would you understand me if I said I have never felt so loved and understood by another person as I did at that moment? It was like he had invented a figure of me from soft wax with his own hands and then handed me that homunculus so I could ask her all of these questions and listen to each of her ingenious new confessions.

Titiba & the Invention
of the Unknown

T he historian Michel de Certeau wants to know what makes ideas possible. He asks versions of the question over and over in *The Writing of History*. "What makes something thinkable?" And insists the answer is the only story historians should bother telling.

> Herrick: Titiba what evil spirit have you familiarity with.
> Titiba: None.
> H: Why do you hurt these children.
> T: I do not hurt them.

Of all the accused witches, Titiba is the one who seems to have been the most radically transformed from who she actually was into who certain people wanted her to be. Unlike the white people of Salem, whose names, lineages, and racial identities have remained fixed since that time, hers went from Titiba in the trial records to Tituba in the popular culture. She was called "Indian" in court, but imagined in the histories that followed as African, African American, and Afro-Caribbean. Henry Wadsworth Longfellow, in *Giles Corey of the Salem Farms*, fictionalized her into "the daughter of a man all black and fierce," while in *The Crucible*, that play performed in high schools all over the country every October, Arthur Miller called into being a reckless storyteller sowing wild fancies in the minds of the village girls.

Glamour, grammar, and grimoire all share the same root. The inquisitors imagined in one testimonial after another that they saw the transformation from person to demon before their eyes, even as they clung more fiercely to the illusion they held about themselves, that they were not the ones conjuring such nightmares. It was Goodwife Sibley who asked Titiba to perform that old English spell with bread, dirt, and urine to ease the suffering of the poor afflicted child Betty, but that moment glimmered back in court as Titiba's idea, her spell, her fault. And though she was compelled by the violence of Samuel Parris's open hand into this line of questions by Constable Joseph Herrick, the dominant narrative that emerged in the historiographies was that her confession was the reason for the craze that followed, that Titiba's words conjured what we would come to know as the Salem Witch Hunt.

H: Who is it then.

T: The devil for ought I know.

H: Did you never see the devil.

T: The devil came to me and bid me serve him.

The Arawak word for the island renamed Barbados in the late fifteenth century is Ichi-rougan-aim, which means red land / island with white teeth. In the Eurocentric propaganda masquerading as so many of the textbooks distributed in history and social studies classes in this country you will read that the Arawak people disappeared or went extinct. In those books you will not read the word "genocide" because "genocide" means a crime was committed. You will not read "survivors" because in an ethical and moral world "survivors" means restitution must still be made. Today more than ten thousand people living in northern coastal regions of South America identify as Lokono, which is the name those people the colonizers called Arawaks used to call themselves.

H: Who have you seen.

T: Four women sometimes hurt the children.

H: Who were they.

T: Goode Osburn and Sarah Good and I do not know who the others were. Sarah Good and Osburne would have me hurt the children but I would not. She further saith there was a tall man of Boston that she did see.

It was with witch trials in mind that Certeau critiqued his profession in his manifesto calling for the creation of new histories. "What we initially call history is nothing more than a narrative," he writes, adding with mounting frustration that "the legend provides the imaginary dimension that we need so that the elsewhere can reiterate the here and now...."

It was with Certeau in mind that I read *Pedagogies of Crossing* by M. Jacqui Alexander, who founded and directs the Tobago Center for the Study and Practice of Indigenous Spirituality. She says that to create a just and sustainable future, we must "destabilize that which hegemony has rendered coherent or fixed; reassemble that which appears to be disparate, scattered, or otherwise idiosyncratic; foreground that which is latent and therefore powerful in its apparent absence; and analyze that which is apparently self-evident, which hegemony casts as commonsensical and natural, but which we shall read as gestures of power, that deploy violence to normalize and discipline."

> H: When did you see them.
> T: Last night at Boston.
> H: what did they say to you.
> T: They said hurt the children
> H: And did you hurt them
> T: No there is 4 women and one man they hurt the children and they lay upon me and they tell me if I will not hurt the children they will hurt me.

Elaine Breslaw, author of *Tituba, Reluctant Witch of Salem*, was the first historian I read who looked through the glamour the inquisitors cast over Titiba and saw instead the resistance she conjured in her testimony. Breslaw speculates that Titiba's name came from the Tivitivas tribe living at the mouth of the Orinoco. Or the Tetebetana community of Arawaks living near the Amacura River. She found

a 1676 inventory of a Barbados plantation owned by Samuel
Thompson in which the name of a child, Tattuba, appears, along
with sixty-six other names of slaves.

The spelling of names and many other words was irregular then,
and the timeline makes sense, particularly given that Samuel Parris
seems to have known the Thompson family well, even lived at
a plantation near theirs in Barbados before setting sail for New
England to take his new position in Salem as the minister of a
rural Puritan community notorious for its squabbles, discord, and
tendency to fire their clergy.

> H: But did you not hurt them
> T: Yes but I will hurt them no more.
> H: Are you not sorry you did hurt them.
> T: Yes.
> H: And why then doe you hurt them.
> T: They say hurt children or wee will doe worse to you.

I'm always surprised by the number of intellectuals I have seen
throw up their hands and say we'll never be able to understand
what happened in Salem or why. It is, after all, fairly identical to
what happened in Bamberg, where three mayors in ten years were
executed as witches along with hundreds of others, not to mention
in Lancashire and Paisley, all across Spain and its colonies, etc.,
etc.— there is the same line of questioning, the fear, and then the
fear, hunger and drought or winter, a fungus, maybe, in the damp

grain which causes delusions, something like what the DSM-5 might call PTSD from the most recent war, gaslighting gaolers and judges, a little torture, then a lot of torture…. In most of the trials you can tell nothing about the lives of the judges or the accused or afflicted or the audience feels sustainable based on how often one person will say and another person will agree that the world is surely ending soon.

And then there is that same old faith. In general the inquisitors won't relent until a confession includes something new. New variations reassure them that they aren't just being told what they want to hear. This is why they torment the accused past mere confession to the point where the trembling person accuses someone else.

So let's observe that Titiba never points the finger at anyone else. This is the only thing about the trials in Salem that is actually unusual at all. When asked who was torturing the girls, Sarah Good said it must be the insufferable Sarah Osbourne. Sarah Osbourne said if anything Sarah Good was the bewitched one and anyway she'd had a dream of being pricked by "something like an Indian." When pressed, Titiba, who was often referred to by her neighbors as "Indian" or "Titiba Indian" named the two already-accused Sarahs, sure—they were already in shackles and accusing each other; what could she do for them? But when asked to name more, she said she could not make out any other names or faces.

H: What have you seen.

T: A man came to me and say serve me.

H: What service.

T: Hurt the children and last night there was an appearance that said kill the children and if I would not go on hurting the children they would do worse to me.

H: What is this appearance you see.

T: Sometimes it is like a hog and sometimes like a great dog, this appearance she saith she did see 4 times.

Historians typically begin the story of Salem in the woods of 1691, where the Reverend Samuel Parris's daughter, Betty, and his niece, Abigail, met to use an old divination method of telling their fortunes with an egg yolk. They expected to see the faces of their future lovers, but instead saw coffins and were not right again. They turned hysterical and began barking like dogs. Later, Abigail was found dancing in those woods.

H: What did it say to you?

T: ... The black dog said serve me but I said I am afraid he said if I did not he would doe worse to me.

H: What did you say to it.

T: I will serve you no longer. then he said he would hurt me and then he looked like a man and threatens to hurt me, she said that this man had a yellow bird that kept with him and he told me he had more pretty things that he would give me if I would serve him.

Because, like Certeau, I have been trying to understand what makes certain ideas thinkable, I have been reading the Situationists between the transcripts of the Salem testimonies and walking a meandering path through my neighborhood, which is a square of unceded Dakota land that was for a time a thriving center of African American businesses, homes, and prosperity. By 1968 urban planners, who were and are overwhelmingly white and male, had poured I-94 directly through the heart of this district on purpose and by design to destabilize the community. They probably did something similar where you live.

In the most anthologized of Situationist texts, "Elementary Program of the Bureau of Unitary Urbanism," the philosophers Attila Kotányi and Raoul Vaneigem write, "Modern capitalism, which organizes the reduction of all social life to a spectacle, is incapable of presenting any spectacle other than that of our alienation."

> H: What were these pretty things.
> T: He did not show me them.
> H: What also have you seen
> T: Two rats, a red rat and a black rat.

Capitalism, it is widely known but seldom said, is dependent on the invention of scarcity. Salem villagers were obsessed with firewood, which had been made very scarce by their overharvesting. As it became clear it would not be so easy to simply spread European colonization north, a three-generations-old feud over a tract of land between the influential Putnam and Proctor families was more and more on everyone's mind. It came up each time the village had to agree to hire or fire a minister, build or not build a new meeting house, issue a warrant for some new arrest. You can grow and then cut down and burn a lot of trees on one thousand disputed acres.

Bur oak, mossy cup oak, yellow oak, chinkapin oak, sandbar willow, swamp birch, Bicknell's hawthorn, mountain winterberry, sweet bay magnolia, swamp cottonwood, northern mountain ash, northern white cedar.

In the negotiations conducted by letters from that Barbados plantation, Samuel Parris had secured a promise of firewood as well as a home to go along with his modest paycheck as part of his contract with the convening members of the church. But when winter arrived, neither the wood nor his paychecks were delivered.

Everyone in that small cold household—his wife, the four children, Titiba and also the other enslaved person, John Indian— lived inside the drafting and revising of the week's sermons, the practicing and polishing of weekly jeremiads that became increasingly preoccupied with an evil that had infected the village.

Would any of them have remembered a view of the indigenous trees of Barbados growing scarce amidst all of the clear-cut sugar plantations stretched out across the island? Changunga, cedro, kapok, guaiacwood, sandbox tree, lemon guava, cabbage palm, false mastic, swizzlestick tree.

> H: What did they say to you.
> T: They said serve me.
> H: When did you see them.
> T: Last night and they said serve me, but I said I would not.

"The functional is what is practical," Kotányi and Vaneigem observe in their Situationist manifesto, in which they try to lay out the core ideas necessary to make thinkable their utopian vision of a new kind of society. "The only thing that is practical is the resolution of our fundamental problem: our self-realization (our escape from the system of isolation)."

Salem was located in the Massachusetts Bay Colony, which was intended by its founders to be a utopia, organized around a deep understanding of all the ways their old home and life had failed them.

To justify the bloodshed their utopia seemed to require, the colonists designed a seal that was a picture of a Native American wearing a loincloth made of leaves with a banner issuing forth from his mouth that reads "Come over and help us." A scapegoating caricature created by the same land- and power-hungry people who conjured the myth of the crone.

H: What service.

T: She said hurt the children.

H: Did you not pinch Elizabeth Hubbard this morning

T: The man brought her to me and made me pinch her

H: Why did you goe to Thomas Putnams last night and hurt his child.

T: They pull and hall me and make me goe

It is all too easy for those who benefit from hegemonic powers to say there is nothing to learn from the uncertainties of these trials. That the mist of spectral evidence clouds all judgement. This is, after all, what the governor eventually said when he issued a general pardon to all of the accused who had not already been executed. But in fact there is a great deal the afflicted know quite well and anyone who cared to could learn.

H: And what would have you doe.

T: Kill her with a knife.

Did you know that Titiba was likely married to John Indian? He also survived the trials. He joined the ranks of the afflicted, trembling and fainting and accusing, which was a clever way then for anyone to stay alive or exact vengeance or both in that strange year. His name was probably not really John Indian. I like to imagine he and Titiba knew each other by the names their mothers or grandmothers or aunts or fathers or brothers or whoever it was loved and cared for them had used at their beginning.

H: How did you go?

T: We ride upon stickes and are there presently.

H: Doe you goe through the trees or over them.

T: We see nothing but are there presently.

H: Why did you not tell your master.

T: I was afraid they said they would cut of[f] my head if I told.

It is unclear precisely how many members of Salem village owned human beings as slaves. The first comprehensive records appear in 1754 when Governor Shirley ordered a census of all slaves over sixteen. In that year there were at least eighty-three people of African or indigenous descent living as property in Salem village.

It is with Certeau and Alexander in mind that I have concluded there is nothing new to learn about history. There is only what I might try once more to see clearly.

H: Would you not have hurt others if you co[u]ld.

T: They said they would hurt others but they could not

When Breslaw tells the story, she emphasizes the resistance in Titiba's description of the nameless and faceless members of a coven, dressed in the fine clothes of well-to-do people. She proposes a new history that explains how a group of people came to have the idea that there is no such thing as witches. Her story goes like this: When a person like Titiba, who is not supposed to know how, masters the system and turns it against those who would master her, the ruling class suddenly and conveniently realizes nothing they have believed makes sense anymore.

> H: What attendants hath Sarah Good.
> T: A yellow bird and shee would have given me one.
> H: What meate did she give it?
> T: It did suck her between her fingers.

Of all the pretty things the devil was said to have promised the people of Salem, my favorite is this yellow bird flying through the ash and charcoal palette of a cold and miserable place.

The yellow birds of Barbados include: yellow-throated vireo, bananaquit, American redstart, American yellow warbler, northern waterthrush, prothonotary warbler, prairie warbler.

Yellow birds that can be found in New England: saffron finch, goldfinch, pine warbler, yellow-throated vireo, yellow-breasted chat, yellow-rumped warbler, yellow-headed blackbird. The recently extincted Bachman warbler would have been there when Titiba was.

> H: Did not you hurt Mr Currins child?
> T: Goode good and goode Osburn told that they did hurt Mr Currens child and would have had me hurt him too, but I did not
> H: What hath Sarah Osburn?
> T: Yellow dog, she had a thing with a head like a woman with 2 legges, and wings. Abigail Williams that lives with her Uncle

Parris said that she did see the same creature, and it turned into
the shape of Goode Osburn.

H: What else have you seen with Osburn?

T: Another thing, hairy it goes upright like a man it hath only
2 legges.

What was known then and is known now, but almost never is
included in the story is that Titiba had a child who was about two
years old when the trials began, just over three years old when it
was over. Her name was Violet.

When the general pardon was issued, the accused only had to pay
their prison costs to be released. Samuel Parris did not pay the seven
pounds owed for Titiba. We know she lived with little food and
little heat in that prison for at least six more months until someone
whose name no one thought to record bought her for the price
of this modest debt. We also know that Violet was never with her
mother again, because in Samuel Parris's will, which was executed
forty-five years later, she was handed down to his heirs.

H: Did you not see Sarah Good upon Elizabeth Hubbard, last
Saturday?

T: I did see her set a wolfe upon her to afflict her, the persons with
this maid did say that she did complain of a wolfe.

T: She further saith that shee saw a cat with good at another time.

H: What cloathes doth the man go in?

T: He goes in black clothes a tall man with white hair I thinke.

H: How doth the woman go?

T: In a white hood and a black hood with a top knot.

H: Doe you see who it is that torments these children now.

At the time of the writing of this essay, the US Immigration and Customs Enforcement agency held an estimated 10,000 migrant children in its custody; at least seven had died. Which is a situation not unlike the one from 1879 to 1918 when the US government took 12,000 children from their parents and their nations or bands into the abusive Carlisle Indian School, an institution that approximately 150 other US-run or Canadian-run or Catholic-run boarding schools for Native children modeled themselves after. Half of the 120,000 people held in Japanese internment camps in the US were children. Of the 12.5 million people carried across the Atlantic during the five centuries of the transatlantic slave trade, 26 percent are estimated to have been children. The number of children born into slavery has not yet been calculated, but they have been there, the children, afflicted, since the beginning of the American story.

T: Yes it is Goode Good, shee hurts them in her own shape

H: And who is it that hurts them now.

T: I am blind now. I cannot see

The Devil's Book

The devil keeps a book of names where you sign in your own blood or some other potioned ink like a liquid iron gall. There is no erasing it, there is no smearing it.

When I try to imagine the devil's book, I see the piled-up files as the historian combs through every record, bill of sale, ship's manifest, and diary, trying to find one enslaved woman's name in that sea of ink. I try again to see his book, but called to mind instead is that scene out of the transcripts of Salem when a judge asked the enslaved woman Candy if she had signed the devil's book. She answered that her mistress had once shown her that her name was written in a book and she felt the presence of a great evil, the kind of thing the Puritans called "the devil." Candy said, "Candy no witch in her country. Candy's mother no witch. Candy no witch, Barbados."

When you decide to discover everything known about the devil's book of names, a great many of the forks in your reading will switchback to Herman, a Czech priest who transcribed and illustrated the *Codex Gigas*. Herman the Recluse, the story goes, not inclined to a life of ascetic restraint, broke his monastic vows and was sentenced to be walled up alive. Frightened and frantic, he promised to create a book in one single night that would glorify the monastery forever and include all human knowledge. At midnight the monk prayed to Lucifer for aid; the devil finished the book in exchange for his soul.

In another version of the story he lived inside that wall for thirty years, atoning for his sins by copying and illustrating.

Elsewhere it is said the abbot gave him a year to glorify the monastery from his tomb and after that he would be walled in and left to starve. At midnight on the last night of the year he made his pact.

It is formally known as the *Codex Gigas* because it is gigantic, the largest book the Holy Roman Empire would know. Medievalists observe how unique it is for its constancy of script. Most illuminated manuscripts were collaborative endeavors among whole monasteries of scribes, but here it really does seem like one man did work that, by the math of the archivists, would have taken approximately thirty years of daylight hours to complete.

It is informally known as the Devil's Book because Folio 290 recto depicts a florid and gleaming devil painted with gilded inks made of liquefied precious gems. The devil hunches in a loincloth, his green face snarls behind a thin and twirling moustache, ruby eyes, and two bloody horns protruding from his temples. His three-toed feet and hands have talons shaped like licks of flame. Sharp dewclaws curve out from his ankles. A dragon, a bird of prey, a snake in one body glowing off the animal-skin page.

A lot of medieval demons you'll see in the marginalia of psalters, Bibles, and books of hours look like caricatures of African people. This one is inspired by the medieval European caricatures to dehumanize Asian people. Freud and other early psychoanalysts spent a lot of time studying cases of demon possession and asking what they tell us about neuroses. But it wasn't until Frantz Fanon and other post-colonial psychoanalysts started to ask what in the history of ideas makes the madness of racism possible that the invention of demons really makes sense.

If your name appears in the devil's book, to hear the Puritans tell it, he is now your master. If they let themselves think very much about it, the Puritans must have been terrified that what they had done to other people might in turn be done to them.

When Nathan Putnam, master of Mary Black, told her in no uncertain terms she was forbidden to confess to anything the court asked, no matter how they pressed, did she appreciate the encouragement to hold fast to truth or just fear his commands more than those of the magistrate?

Unlike Mary Black, the enslaved woman Candy confessed and she also accused. "Candy no witch, Barbados." She said, "In this country mistress give Candy witch." When the magistrates asked how her mistress made her a witch, Candy answered, "Mistress bring book and pen and ink, make Candy write in it." The historian Cassander L. Smith lingers over the forty words of hers in this fragmented slip of a trial record we have left from that moment. Smith sees in her testimony an "instance of verbal resistance" when Candy "circumscribed the transcriber's (and court prosecutors') own rhetorical strategies" and makes us think about who her mistress really is, of what she is capable, and what it means to see your name written on someone else's pages. She makes those who would have dismissed her as nothing more than property consider what it makes you when you say you have the papers to prove you own someone's soul. The records say that the afflicted Puritans in the room, upon hearing Candy's words and then seeing her dunk some knotted rags in a bucket, "were greatly affrighted and fell into violent fits."

The truth is here and has been the whole time. Even, or perhaps especially, pathological liars get their tongues all tied up in it. Medieval Christians called this phenomenon the Anti-Christ—every good has its opposite, every Christ his Satan, every Bible its Devil's Book, every congregation its coven. They preferred to imagine that opposite existed outside themselves. It was only when they looked back on his life that the brothers came to call Herman a recluse. Recluse, so they wouldn't instead have to say how they sealed a man into a dark room with just a small slit of light through which food and waste and paper and ink passed in and out. What a relief it must have been, to imagine that it was the devil in there looking out at you, and not a glimpse of yourself looking in.

Horseshoes

After dumping the burned remains of the Paisley witches in their mass grave at a crossroads, authorities sealed it with a horseshoe that sits now in the center of a traffic circle, cars whizzing around. Unlike most of the recorded executions, where the women were compliant, apologetic, and pleading, Catherine Campbell struggled and screamed all the way to the gallows. She called down the wrath of God and the devil on her accusers. Then Agnes Naismith was dragged to the scaffold. Before she was hanged then burned, she laid what she called a dying woman's curse on the town. Some residents of Paisley say, despite the iron meant to hold an evil thing down, they can still feel those women's angry heat.

Paisley, an old mill town of mostly shuttered factories, is not so different from where I sit now. Potosi, Missouri, named after the mythical city of precious minerals the conquistadors set forth to claim, is one of many villages born of metals colonizers came here to dig and mine and smelt. Down the road is Old Mines, over the valley from Steelville, in a watershed with Leadwood, across a dry river from the Iron County line.

One wonders what possessed the people who made the accusations, and how they lived with themselves after. There are a few instances of regret and recantation—after what she helped make possible in Salem, Ann Putnam insisted her body be buried in an unmarked grave. She said, "I desire to lie in the dust, and to be humble for it, in that I was a cause, with others, of so sad a calamity to them and their families; for which cause I desire to lie in the dust, and earnestly beg forgiveness of God."

Christian Shaw's testimony led to the execution of Catherine Campbell, Agnes Naismith, and others—seven people in all, including John and James Lindsay, brothers aged eleven and fourteen, who died on the scaffold holding each other's hands. And yet she has no such apology on record. She was eleven when she saw her servant Catherine steal a drink of milk. She told her mother what the maid had done, and Catherine, pissed off at the stinginess of the whole household, cursed the girl, saying she wished the devil would "haul her soul through Hell." Not long after, Christian encountered old, trembling, much-whispered-about Agnes Naismith on the road. Soon the girl was having fits and seizures, feelings of flying through the air, and coughing up bits of hair, charcoal, chicken feathers, and straw. The usual symptoms.

It is possible Christian Shaw was a murderous, conniving psychopath. Others have suggested we might attribute cases like hers to what the DSM-5 calls functional neurological symptom disorder. There are experts who say it is worth considering the possibility that witchcraft is real, especially to those who believe in it. So far as we know, the girl herself never wondered whether the story of her life was a delusion or a sin or a convenient occasion for landed gentry to demonstrate their power. She was after all the daughter of the Laird of Bargarran, and the daughters of lairds seldom have to contemplate, must less justify, the reasons for or the consequences of their actions.

I read these accusations and convictions, recantations and curses beside a stream that flows through a water table the lead mines bought the underground rights to back in the Depression years, one desperate farmer at a time. Out here some of the water runs clear some of the time. Anymore you never know when the mines might sink a spring or let it run a kind of slurry through the mess of what they do underneath us. When there's work, my kin cut steel, my kin weld iron, my kin go into the lead mines. When there is not work, my kin collect scrap metal, my kin sell, my kin cook, my kin become the cops who arrest them and the prison guards who hold them for it. Out here there is the highest incidence of lead poisoning per capita in children anywhere other than Flint.

Centuries before Agnes Naismith was hung by a rope and then burned at the stake, Saint Dunstan, the tenth-century farrier and owner of a great iron forge, was asked by the devil to shoe his cloven hoof. Dunstan recognized his customer and agreed, but then caused him so much pain digging the nails into the most tender places he could reach, the devil begged him leave off. Dunstan stopped his work on the promise the devil would never again enter a place where a horseshoe was hung.

Among other things, the Paisley witches were accused of discovering you can hang the horseshoe over your threshold upside down and your presser, your cold-shoe, your mare ride, your sphinx moth, your sweetest sin, your siren song would not be thwarted entry.

This newborn creek is so clear we can watch trout, old and huge as river gods, graze past the green grasses ten feet deep before spilling downstream to discover the silt runoff and limestone bottoms of our careworn hills. The people my ancestors drove away, starved out, murdered in cold blood, or just never spared a single thought for at all, members of the Osage Nation called and call this place sacred. Because there is no place we can go where we do not carry our history and because there is no place where we will allow each other to speak of it either, we eat beside the ruins of the forges where iron ore was mined and then carted down the hill to be cast into bullets during the Civil War, for whichever side wanted to pay the highest price. Though I wish it were otherwise, I know I am surrounded by people who hope it was the Confederacy that made the best use of them.

The horseshoe, because Mars, the God of War and Warhorses, was an enemy of Saturn, the Liege Lord of Witches.

"Close only counts in horseshoes and hand grenades," we say out here with derision and cruelty when someone who has lost something tries to offer a reason why.

There is an old admonition to put a horseshoe on your stable to keep the evil things from stealing milk from your cows or leaving your horses exhausted and covered with sweat. But the crumble-down barns are empty except for the rats and possums and the dusty piles of feces they leave in the stalls of their wake.

Out here white people forget what they know as a way to live with it. If you have a hilltop your great-great-granddaddy handed down, you'll dig up a century's worth of shotgun shells when you disc the wheat, and then arrowheads, a coin or two a conquistador would have held between his fingers. You'll disc up bones and some of them will be human. And if all you have is a bank account left behind with your family's name on it, it's even easier to refuse to remember what horror it took and takes to be here.

Christian Shaw grew up. She traveled widely across Europe with her mother, who was also her business partner. After finding such fine thread being spun in Holland, they smuggled pieces of that new invention, the spinning jenny, back home in their skirts. And then founded Bargarran Threads, which would become the industrial backbone of Paisley's mill-town economy for the next four hundred years. Whether Christian felt like a survivor of something terrible or a murderer of the innocent or just never thought of anyone but herself at all is impossible to say for certain.

Who remembers now that before there was the word nightmare, there were the stories of the mara, those dreadful harriers of horse flesh and dreams?

The mara, those white-mothed souls of people who leave their bodies in the night.

The mara, who sit astride your chest and ride you through your dreams so hard you wake each morning in a pant.

In the old legends a Viking invader called Thorkel the Tall once had a dream about riding a red mare that barely touched ground. He thought it a positive omen, but his wife knew the red foretold blood and the mare was the self of himself he was about to lose.

Locked out here with the ghosts of those who tied the rope, lit the match, plunged the shovel, clamped shut their mouths, squeezed tight their eyes.

The mara ride you so fast you could catch your own reflection.

The mara ride until you beg for a horseshoe to hold the flying winds of yourself down.

When the mara's hooves thunk across the lead, it rings a steely echo.

Glas Gaibhleann

The people were obsessed with milk. The people were obsessed with ways to stop the witches from stealing the milk. So great was their obsession that the *Malleus Maleficarum*, that handbook for inquisitors, devoted an entire chapter to the subject under the heading "Here followeth how witches injure cattle in various ways."

The witches, it was said, make a thing called a tilberi. First they steal a rib from a recently buried body, then wind it up in wool stolen from beneath the shoulders of a widow's sheep. They tuck it between their breasts and for the next three Sundays at Communion they spit sanctified wine on the thing, watching it grow more alive with each spit. When grown enough, it sucks the inside of a thigh. And when it is finally weaned, it can be sent to steal milk. Each night it returns to call at the window, "Full belly, Mommy," and vomit the stolen milk into a butter churn.

The witches turn into rabbits and suckle the cow's teat, they turn into butterflies and their fluttering sours the cream. They turn into owls or flies or dogs or cats for the sake of creeping on that milk. They call it through spells into their own pails. They ask and then torment anyone who will not give a glass.

They make a hair rope by knotting severed cows' tails and then tugging that rope while repeating the charm:

> Cow's milk and mare's milk
> and every beast that bares milk
> between St. Johnstone's and Dundee
> Come 'a to me, come 'a to me.

Before there was "nature" as a concept separate from "the world"; before there were sugar plantations and coffee plantations and tobacco fields stretched out to the horizon; before there were cotton gins working their gears as fast as a pair of scarred and aching hands could feed them, there was the story of Glas Gaibhleann and the beginning of milk.

The history of milk is a history of unexpected gifts and unexpected consequences. Though relatively common among those of European descent, lactase persistence is a genetic abnormality that allows adult bodies to process lactose. Just a one-standard-deviation increase in the emergence of this genetic variation is associated with a 40 percent rise in population density as milk's fats, proteins, vitamins, and minerals added balance to precolonial diets, creating economic and population booms. Followed only later by the density corrections of famine, war, and plague.

Before there were witches or demons or God the Father in His Heavens, before telescopes or microscopes or manuscripts were carried across those mountains that divided the monasteries of Europe from the libraries of the Middle East, before the priests began to tremble at the smallest voice in their heads wondering if . . . , the people told how Glas Gaibhleann, the divine cow, gave a rich cream and her udders never ran dry. She could walk the island of the world in a single day. The rocky Burren was made by her hooves and she fed all whom she met. No one ever starved when she was around.

So of course the people tried to enslave her and take her abundance for themselves. When she left for the stars, only that creamy sheen of the Milky Way was left behind.

The history of witches is a history of need. You can see this by how people are always accusing witches of stealing the milk. The history of witches is also the history of a social contract. You can see this by how people sometimes went to the witches for medicine to keep themselves alive and sometimes pointed an accusing finger to keep themselves alive. When you are afraid, it can be difficult not to hate the people you need. Sometimes I think I am the one calling it all into my pail. Sometimes I think I am the mob. Sometimes I think none of it is real except the fear.

And sometimes I'm miles outside the town of my life, watching the butterflies pollinate the fields of flowers the rabbits dash and hunker. Any of these could be a witch carrying a mouthful of buttercream. This whole mountain might be nothing but small and large sips of milk that have been stolen or borrowed or brought back home to share. Surely this too could be a place where that great cow once put down a hoof.

Hildegard von Bingen

Despite the obvious similarities and the fact she was summoned to an inquisition, Hildegard von Bingen was not a witch, she was a canonized saint. Her epiphanic hallucinations are gathered into one text, *Scivias,* her remedies for ailments (collected from Persian translations in her convent library and folklore from the fields beyond the cloister garden walls) are kept separate in *Physica.* As if they have nothing to do with each other.

The *Physica* reads like one of the more beautiful spell books I've seen.

"Whoever is plagued by wrong dreams should have betony leaves close by when going to sleep."

"If anyone have a headache, and his head is buzzing as if he were deaf, let him eat often of cloves, and they will ameliorate the buzzing in his head."

"If any have a weak and sad heart, let him cook mullein with meat or fish … and it will strengthen his heart and make it merry."

Like some member of the Heresy of the Free Spirit, a movement she inspired that arose a century later and provoked a great deal of burning, I've been having erotic fantasies about the divine. Specifically, the emerald Hildegard kept beside her bed as a symbol or a touchstone or a threshold to the green soul of this world. Also, it was, she said, an aid and remedy to the seizures that accompanied her visions.

Last night, for example, I was walking in the little forest in the center of our city and having the feeling of ecstasy and yearning I get in equal measures any time I go to the woods. I feel opened up and rushing, as if there were a wound like a river in my chest and I think I just need to channel it somewhere so it won't feel so much like I am the wound splintering that river.

I'm sorry to say this, but a husband you've known for practically your whole life who is off driving a bus somewhere to make money for the car payment, who needs an Excedrin every morning and didn't particularly care for the grilled fish you made last night either but sure he'll pick up some shampoo on the way home, he's just not really working as a destination for this particular stream of great and terrible.

I wonder on these walks if this means I don't love him at all or enough or where I could ever find a place to take this cup of wracking feeling that makes it hard to eat, and pour it out.

What I mean is that I've been wondering if this feeling of the forest beating my heart horny is a way of being called back to the Church. There is a green part of the Church, after all, with the liturgical seasons and a different plant under the bare feet of each saint in the book and all those candles of women singing "Ave Maria."

"If a man have any rotten flesh in him, then boil this herb [vervain] in water, lay a linen cloth on his wounds, and when the water has been pressed out lay on the vervain too. Do this until all the rottenness is gone."

"If a man is forgetful and would be cured of it, let him crush out the juice of the stinging nettle, and add some olive oil, and when he goes to bed, let him anoint his chest and temples with it and do this often, and his forgetfulness will be alleviated."

"Lavender wine will provide a person with pure knowledge and a clear understanding."

I've been walking past the white stones of Sacred Heart each morning on the way home. I've been telling myself it's a form of field research. So far I have not forgotten how the place remains mortared up with black-frocked priests and the chinks all stuffed with papal bulls.

I try not to think too much about the theology classes I was required to take year after year and how the nuns went on about *agape*, or divine love, as superior to the erotic. That was the line they used to get all the cool seniors to take pledges of secondary virginity and how they got the rest of us to feel smug about everything we didn't know. I don't appreciate having been so manipulated and don't intend to succumb to so much rhetoric twice.

After spending a great many years pretending to feel the things everybody else claims to be feeling in the measure they claim to feel them, now I feel like thinking about how Hildegard holds that emerald in her mouth. It is as green as the moisture of the body, she says, as the rain that falls down into the earth and smooth as glass when I run my mouth along the worn edges of the rough cut.

She explained her visions as an arrival of light, rooted in the green of the soul, which glows as the leaves glow after a rain when the sun is bright and every droplet becomes a convex mirror. "Then the greenness of the earth and the grasses thrives with the greatest vigor," she says. "For the air is still cold and the sun is already warm. The plants suck the green life force as strongly as a lamb sucks its milk."

I started reading about witches because I thought I'd find people talking about how they felt this green world offering to take over their bodies if only they could figure out how to let it. But what I found was just the usual politics and patriarchal bullshit. Much like how I started a garden, but your own garden is never as beautiful as someone else's patch of weeds, much as your own food is never as delicious as a meal cooked by someone else, and the sex is never quite what you thought it would be when you are the one choreographing it.

Of course it's an old theme to suggest that the intellect and the erotic are born of the same seed. After all, the thinking goes, the desire to know is, first and foremost, a desire to sense. If you ask Foucault, he'll say Aristotle thought it first, though it is Foucault's explanation that rings like a vision—"the desire to know was inscribed in nature, *phusei*, it is now presented as the pleasure of the sensation taken in itself, i.e. apart from any utility." It gets hotter. "There are as many distinct pleasures as there are activities of sensation." And, climactically, "Desire is knowledge deferred, but made visible in the impatience of the suspense in which it is held."

Like anybody, I live at the intersection of longing and discipline. Like anybody, I am not sure if I have made the right choices.

Hildegard was reluctant to speak of or write her visions. She waited for the bishops to badger her for an accounting. And then she only offered it in Latin, not like those careless heretics proclaiming what they had seen in those vulgar tongues that people pushing their carts along the roads could understand. She reminds me of my friend whose strategy for keeping her sensations real is to hardly ever tell them to anyone else. Like Foucault explaining Socrates, this friend and this saint of mine each believe in "a knowledge which bewitches and whose gaze dazzles on those whom it fixes." Sometimes she graces me with one of her secrets as a way of showing our friendship is important to her. Once she gave me the secret that she likes to scatter her secrets among friends so no one person knows everything. As in, "Oedipus does not look at the secret but the secret looks at him, it does not take its eyes off him."

When I think about what others might call a sin, I think of it as research. I think of it as *Causae et Curae*. I think of how I need to know what it is between us, me and my longing, me and anyone, me and the mystery of this world that surrounds us. I think of it as fennel and that "however fennel is eaten, it makes men merry, and gives them a pleasant warmth, and makes them sweat well, and causes good digestion."

The Aristotles that Never Were

When I am thinking about leaving my husband, my friend reminds me of that poem we both like where you sit and watch the boats on the horizon that are all the lives you might have lived.

When I am trying to decide what I want out of the realm of what's possible, I watch a hummingbird pollinate the fireweed as he does every morning of this season and think about how Aristotle said all knowledge is rooted in the senses. How he said philosophy begins with our own desire to feel because we cannot know anything until we know why we feel what we feel and do not what we do not.

Aristotle's name and writings disappeared for centuries. Arabic librarians were the ones that saved him until the Crusaders came and wanted their literacy back. But translation creates infinite possible meanings in a pool with the ripple of infinite ways to say them. Whales surface and propagate the mysterious science of their deep being out at the horizon where they are almost, or perhaps are, or most certainly are not, more of those pretty white sails.

Pseudo-Aristotelian texts abounded throughout the Middle Ages and the Renaissance. Everybody's favorite handbook for sex and midwifing, *Aristotle's Masterpiece*, was just one of the manuscripts inappropriately credited to him, who would probably not have proposed hirsute maidens and dark-skinned infants were the consequences of their parents' imaginations at the moment of conception.

There was also not-Aristotle's *De proprietatibus elementorum*, a work on geology that was considered helpful by the alchemists. And *On the Universe* was a popular reference for the astrologers that Aristotle did not write. Real Thomas Aquinas read and appreciated Unreal Aristotle's *The Book of Aristotle's Explanations of Pure Good*. If only the *Secreta Secretorum*, a study on the unseen world, had been written by a philosopher who believed your senses, not your mind, determine what is real, then there might be some hope amidst all of our longing.

In *Aristotle's Problemata*, another of these anonymous not-Aristotles asks question after question for hundreds of pages. *What is carnal reproduction?* he wants to know. And, *How are hermaphrodites begotten?*

> *Why is it the change of seasons and the winds intensify or stop diseases and bring them to a crisis and engender them?*

Why do they say a change of drinking water is unhealthy, but not a change of air?

Why do those who are asleep perspire more freely?

Why has wine the effect both of stupefying and of driving to frenzy those who drink it?

Why are the drunken more easily moved to tears?

As I read, I sometimes think Pseudo-Aristotle is paying very close attention and sometimes I think that he pays no attention at all. As I read, my friend is watching the boats. Surely one of them is meant for us.

Why are the melancholic particularly inclined for sexual intercourse?

Why are birds and men with thick hair lustful?

Why are riders on horseback less likely to fall?

Why do some unpleasant sounds make us shudder?

Why is it that some animals cough, while others do not?

I wonder what makes a person so good at noticing questions. It is a gift, I think, to know this art of opening up the ends of ideas and

making them wonder their theories right off into unwritten silence
at the margins of the page.

Why is it that fair men and white horses usually have grey eyes?

Why is it that eunuchs do not become bald?

Why is it that the deaf always speak through their nostrils?

Why are sounds more audible at night?

*Why does cold water poured out of a jug make a shriller sound than hot
water poured out of the same jug?*

I have been admonished about the tedium of going on about
wonder for no other reason than to say "Look how wide my
eyes are right now," but sometimes I just want to tell someone
something amazing I have learned because knowing it has made
me feel happy in a way that being astonished feels happy. I want
the life where someone is happy just to be sitting next to me. I
want the life where I am astonished by unexpected compliments
or a certain way a friend has of finding a reason that is no good
reason to touch my wrist.

Why is the sound of weeping shrill, whereas that of laughing is deep?

Why are our voices deeper in winter?

Why does salt make a noise when it is thrown on the fire?

Why does the voice tremble in those who are afraid?

Why are the odors both of burnt perfumes and flowers less pleasant at a short distance?

Are scents smoke or air or vapor?

Pseudo-Aristotle only answers questions with more questions. Reading his *Problemata* feels like reading the invention of a hypothesis that might one day come to be called the scientific method.

I want our boat-spackled horizon filled with all of the questions I have no idea how to answer. I don't like how we're never going to know the answers, but I like knowing it together. What would Aristotle himself have thought if he knew what was to become of his name? On the truly terrible days, I can only imagine him feeling indifference, as if a fog never lifted and the chair beside him is empty now. As if he never saw his other lives passing by. But that's just one boat. On others he is frustrated by the obfuscation of his work. Or outraged. Or cracking up at what time can do with what we thought we know.

Why is it the bases of bubbles in water are white, and if they are placed in the sun they do not make any shadow, but, while the rest of the bubble casts a shadow, the base does not do so, but is surrounded on all sides by sunlight?

Why is it that the parts of plants and of animals which have no functional importance are round?

Why are contentious disputations useful as a mental exercise?

Why is it that in contentious disputations no trifling can ever occur?

Why do we feel more pleasure in listening to narratives in which the attention is concentrated on a single point than in hearing those which are concerned with many subjects?

Why do those that are grieving and those who are enjoying themselves alike have the flute played to them?

Why is it that of all things which are perceived by the senses that which is heard alone possesses moral character?

Things could be so different from how they are. We cannot say that they would be better. But the possibility of some other way makes this one feel faint and fading and transparent when it could be milky or milky when it could be transparent.

Why do waves sometimes begin to move before the wind reaches them?

Why is it that the waves do not ripple in the deep open sea?

Why is it that if anything is thrown into the sea when it is rough, a calm ensues?

Why is the sea more transparent than fresh water, although it is thicker?

Why is the sea combustible?

Why does the air not become moist when it comes in contact with the water?

Why is it that air is denser than light, but it can pass through solids?

Why is it that air cannot saturate anything?

When I am being melodramatic about my choices, I don't know why we have sensations of choosing in the first place. Why should every minute of our lives be a choice? Is it the case that to choose is to feel yourself pseudoing into some other air or some other sea? When I'm being melodramatic, I feel like I'm multiplying. Aristotle lived for sixty-two years. The child he raised lived for less. The years went by and by. So many people loved so many people in the meantime that the air grew thick with the Pseudo-Aristotles of them all. They became the air we breathe, an atmosphere that could or could not pass through certain metallic solids and certain gelatinous moistures, all of which, like us, are living out lives in suspension.

Agnes Sampson, the Wise Wife of Keith

The definition of a comedy, historically and theoretically, is "any play that ends with a wedding." This is because a wedding is a restoration of the social order, a promise that all the hijinks and shenanigans, the well-bred daughters running away, the well-bred sons putting on women's clothes and falling in love with each other in an act that made it seem like these characters at last were finding a way to be who they are, all that chaos, don't worry, was nothing but a joke.

When I got married in that ridiculous dress while people I hardly knew were crying all around me, it felt like a comedy. But then I always prefer tragedies, which are typically defined by how a new king steps over all of the old king's bodies to assume the throne. Tragedies have their place, because there are times a person needs to cry their guts out and believe this crying has nothing to do with their own selves.

Everyone in that garden said our wedding was like a fairy tale. I agreed, thinking how much a fairy tale can be like a handbook for how to get by within a given social order, with only a minimal undercurrent of grumbling.

Witches, as we know them, were first so characterized in *Macbeth*, a play about a tragic marriage and a fairy tale about the invention of a good king. It has many plot points in common with the life of King James, who assumed the throne of England the year this play was produced. James's father was murdered, his mother was blamed, he believed in the occult, and fretted, as all kings do, that the air was teeming with the wishes of the people around him to see him dead.

For some reason it's not enough for a king to own us, he also has to marry and produce heirs in a fashion that restores our faith in true love and happy endings. No doubt this has to do with some bullshit about the divine rights of kings and perfection of God's plan. In what was described as "the only romantic gesture of his life," young James set sail through a season of devastating storms to collect in person his bride, Princess Anne of Denmark, who had been shipwrecked on the coast of Norway. How people must have swooned to hear of the courage of their king. How the king must have swooned to imagine his own courage while he was doing it.

At this point James was still a skeptic, but he nodded along politely when the in-laws tried to explain away those storms. "These were not signs from God against the marriage!" everyone insisted, as if someone had suggested they might be. "It was devil's work." The Minister of Finance, who, it was whispered in some corners, had inadequately equipped the ships, suggested they hold an inquisition, like a kind of wedding present. He suggested they start by questioning Karen the Weaver, who was known to hold a grudge and was conveniently situated several rungs beneath him on the social ladder.

The proclamations and executions came quickly: Karen the Weaver had sent demons and witches floating across the waters in empty barrels. When they reached the princess's fleet, they climbed up the keel of her ship and summoned the bad weather. But their attempt to thwart the will of God would fail thanks to the vigilant fires of the faithful.

Meanwhile I wonder about Princess Anne and how eager she really was to join James in Scotland. An English spy reported to his majesties that prior to the wedding Anne was "so far in love with the King's Majesty as it were death to her to have it broken off and hath made good proof of divers ways of her affection which his Majestie is apt in no way to requite." The insinuation here is that the Scottish king preferred men. This is the kind of rumor that was sometimes true and sometimes used in a homophobic society to undermine an enemy. Anne was devotedly embroidering shirts for her fiancé while three hundred tailors worked on her wedding dress. This was the kind of gesture that was sometimes true and sometimes used to seal a political alliance. It is hard to say which was the case in this instance, since the way you interpret love letters and rumors five hundred years after the fact says more about you than it could ever say about history.

Some things I could say about the letters and rumors: trying on the dresses is so boring, so too the flowers and the speeches and the long walk down the aisle and interminably being stared at by people who want to believe in what you represent. There was hail clattering the glass roof of the greenhouse chapel so loudly you could hardly hear the string quartet. I liked that part. And I liked that when it was over my mother was happy, my father was happy, and so far as I could tell no one would ever have a reason to demand an explanation for my choices again.

One way of thinking about a wife is that she is more or less invisible and so more or less free, provided she can remember to keep her head down long enough to stay that way.

On the voyage back to Scotland there were more storms. Perhaps the king had really come to believe demonology was a branch of theology. Or perhaps diplomacy required him to take the weather as seriously as Anne's family had and launch a parallel inquisition of his own.

The Newes from Scotland is the pamphlet commissioned by the king to tell the proceedings of the North Berwick witch trials. Here, as in all other trials, name leads unto tortured name until you can hardly remember who accused who. Euphemia Maclean was accused of accepting pain relief from her midwife, Agnes Sampson, who gave her an unspecified powdered substance, a bored stone to keep under her pillow, and some "inchantit mwildis," which are the finger, toe, and knee joints of a disinterred corpse. She was also instructed to put her husband's shirt under the bed during her labor. The part about the shirt seems sweet to me, a kind of tender comfort from a man in this era of rigid gender divisions, but that is probably just one of my happy memories talking. The judges were not touched by it at all—for these things Euphemia Maclean was burned.

In a fairy tale a dangerous woman with power turns a man into the most beastly version of himself. A beautiful, silent, and perfectly stupid girl waits patiently to be taken by him. And then we all live once more happily ever after. In a witch trial you hear a version of this story over and over again. More than three hundred times in James's North Berwick trials.

In comedies women dress and then behave as men, men dress as asses, everyone falls asleep drugged by fairies in the forest. And when they wake to be married, each according to their station, that is meant to feel to the audience, after so much madness, like a choice made freely. All reports indicate Queen Anne and King James got along for the first few years. Then James sent their newborn son away to be raised by his former nurse under the supervision of various trusted lords in a distant castle. It was understood his mother would not see him again until he was a man. This was Scottish royal tradition, but the queen from Denmark was furious and fought to get her son back like a mother who truly loved her child. She attempted both kidnappings and coups. She had many miscarriages that were attributed to her grief and fury.

I like to think Anne was pragmatic from the beginning. I like to think she arrived in Scotland with a packet of seeds a midwife gave her for birth control and this was how she made sure she never lost another child. I like to think no one ever even thought to utter the name of the queen's cunning woman. But what I like to think is not about history or about truth, it is about my love affair with uncovering a well-kept secret that the world might be more just than it seems on its face.

The king and queen began as young as a fairy tale. They grew old and weathered as a scaffold. This was something they did both together and separately.

Agnes Sampson, known by all of her patients and clients as the Wise Wife of Keith, was famous for the help she could offer women who wanted children, women who didn't, women in love, and women in pain. When the king decided he wanted to interrogate this "wise wife" personally, she had been shaved bald, tortured with a rope around her neck for an hour after being pinned to a wall for days by the witch's bridle, which is an iron muzzle with a bit to hold down a woman's tongue. Sampson began at last to speak after her naked body was inspected and a suspicious mark that was said to be the place where the devil put his tongue was found on her privates.

This is almost always the way in witch trials — once the witch knows her mark has been seen, she gives up hope she'll ever slip away from this. She may as well help her inquisitors plan that long walk to the altar. Agnes Sampson confessed so rapidly and so much — a dead cat was thrown in the sea, there was some kind of spell involving the "chiefest parte" of a dead man, a black toad hung up by his heels, this peasant woman, that peasant woman — the king said he could hardly believe her.

With one eye on the instruments hanging from the wall of her cell, she took the king aside and "declared unto him the very words which had passed between the King's majesty and his Queen the first night of their marriage." After that James "wondered greatly, and swore by the living God, that he believed all of the devils in Hell could not have discovered the same."

To this day none of the rest of us knows what these words were. They might have been sweetly romantic or frankly political. You could try to remember the words that passed on the first night of your marriage or the words you would say if you were to do it all over again. But you would have to conclude there is no way to know what love and marriage are to a person who is, as much as any of us can be, living a life that is also an emblem for others.

From the Wise Wife of Keith the king learned two hundred more names in the coven, including that of James Fian, a schoolmaster and the rare male sorcerer, who would soon enough become another subject tortured into confession. He told his crimes like an old tale: Once upon a time he had tried to use a spell to make a woman love him back. He sent a pupil to get the young woman's hair, but her mother intervened and sent the little boy back with hairs from the udder of a cow, which is how he came to be followed everywhere by a lovesick bovine.

Surely the children he taught would have laughed at this punch line the first time he told the story. It seems unlikely that the inquisitor laughed, since Fian's legs were crushed in a contraption called The Bootes the next time he told it.

The character of a king is a way of believing things happen for a reason. The queen is a way of being angry at someone besides God. A witch is a woman who thought her story ended with that wedding a dozen pages back and now she'd be allowed to do as she pleased.

I wonder which of these I would have been and I wonder which I am now. I might have fallen in love, I might have been burned, I might have given up the name of my own dear friend, I might have set the hour of execution, might have pulled the fingernails, might have set the pins, might have been pregnant, might have lost my child, I might have looked around at all I owned and wondered how I could ever hold on to it all. I might walk past those bodies hanging in the town square and know they are intended to mean something to me, but, head down, I have this cart to drag miles yet through the rock and mud before I can warm my hands by a fire, the one my husband is feeding with small sticks even now and thinking how soon I'll be home. I might be the one who tells this story when I get there, but if I have any sense at all, you can be sure the tale will end on a note of how happily, how wise, how just everything turned out in the end.

The Invention of Familiars

S ome things we don't care to talk about by name. It's an
old problem and one of its consequences has been fiction.
Another popular solution is to fill in the gap with an animal.

The monks of the Middle Ages, denying themselves everything a
body wants, or lying about it, were the great theologians of allegory.
From *Animals with Human Faces*, an encyclopedic investigation of
what meant what: "The brute creation, like the world itself, existed
solely for the spiritual edification of man. While animals shared in
the Fall, they had no part in the great plan of Redemption."

The breath of the panther is so sweet that it attracts all animals except
the dragon.

The stag is the enemy of the snake.

The hyena feeds on corpses until its stomach is blown up like
a drum.

In my neck of the woods, where the panther is long extinct and no one's ever even seen a monastery, the saying goes that you'll never see a blue jay on a Friday because that is the day he flies down to hell to give a grain of sand to the devil.

The lion's cubs are born dead and brought to life by the gentle licking of their parents.

The lynx's urine turns into carbuncles in seven days.

No one knows what the devil wants with the blue jay's sand, but in all the stories that bird is good at inventing trouble and good at charming his way around it. Like as not, it is the devil doing Friday penance to the jay and not the other way around.

Certainly the blue jay's tricks and charms would have worked on me. I've always had a thing for a sad-eyed sonofabitch. I'd follow a blue jay to the deserts of hell if he'd let me even try to keep up.

Up here, on the living side of earth, I watch the people falling in love catch and release doves to prove how full their livers are with the humors of passionate devotion. Suckers. Falling for a love that has no grit and songs with no bark.

The beaver, pursued by the hunter, bites off its own testicles and casts them before his predator. The beaver, pursued by a second hunter, rears upright and reveals the empty place of its old genitals.

Once the mole was a magic animal, able to predict the future. "If a man eats the heart of a Mole newly taken out of her belly and panting," the monks said, "he shall be able to devine and foretell infallible events."

As with humans, there was a time when the mole's heart lived not in her chest but in her stomach. It did not beat down there, but panted.

The ram is an icon of brutal, fecund love.

The human race is descended from a wolf.

A blue jay does nothing all day but make deals and exercise his wit. A blue jay will run even the harmless chickadee back to her brush.

A widow of a copyhold tenant could keep her lands, provided she was chaste. Should it be otherwise, she could regain her rights by riding into the court of the manor backwards on a ram, holding its tail between her hands as she recited: "Here I am riding upon a black ram, like a whore as I am."

In the beginning mermaids were saviors and sirens were tempt-resses. One was a fish and one was a bird. Later their features became confused—they might all be women, part fish, part fowl, or even part horse. Any one of them might do anything.

The weasel can kill the basilisk. She has knowledge of the herb of life. She can become a beautiful girl to marry and then, at the wedding feast, revert to her animal nature and pursue a mouse.

This time when the blue jay came back, the poison oak was in bloom and bees were gathering all of the nectar. The lovers were dead and their birds all flown, honey was bitter, and his favorite berries would soon be ripe. A blue jay will make you remember you are just a person and your heart is never going to be anywhere except behind your ribs. I had had my fill. So he sat in his tree alone and barked to anyone who might bother to listen that with himself he was most extremely pleased.

Maria Gonçalves Cajada & the Invention of Love Spells

aria Gonçalves Cajada, the accused sorceress from colonial Brazil, once said, "If the bishop has a mitre, I have a mitre, and if the bishop preaches from the pulpit, I preach from the cadeira." Also, she was widely rumored to feed the devil flesh from a persistent wound on her foot, which is gross, but the sore was the source of her power.

Her life was on the southern coast, but I read about her to the north, driving a narrow peninsula of mountains into that same sea. A whale we saw surface in the far distance of those cold waters would have floated and spumed her coast months before. In the car with a friend who also shocks with the directness of her questions and her demands, I heard myself say what I hadn't know I'd been thinking. "I'm going to leave him."

Back in the seventeenth century, which these currents and the secret creatures of their infinite depths also touched, demonologists and inquisitors were concluding, "Women witches, because of the pact they have made with the Devil, can give news of what is happening at sea or at the ends of the earth." It was not uncommon then to hear that shipwrecked men had fallen into the arms of witches flying over the waters. It was thought that one could find in the sea "the demonological learnings of an entire people: the hazardous labor of ships, dependence on the stars, hereditary secrets, estrangement from women—the very image of the great, turbulent plain itself makes men lose faith in God and all his attachment to his home; he is then in the hands of the Devil, in the sea of Satan's ruses." Among the powers listed in these records kept by the Portuguese inquisitors during their Visitation to the Brazilian colonies was that Maria Gonçalves Cajada could summon storms forcing a ship to port on the pirate islands, using her beloved devil and for the price of two cruzados.

Shipwrecks notwithstanding, the main business of a Brazilian witch was love spells, which formed an important industry in colonial Brazil's underground economy. No records of Maria Gonçalves Cajada's methods are extant, but we have Portuguese accounts of other witches reported to be very good and reliable with their work. One used the native herb supora-mirim and the native bird bemtevi, which is of the tyrant flycatcher family, whose males are known for being constant and protective parents. Their call translates as "I see you well." To attract faithfully married men to her desperate clients, a witch would recite:

Bemtevi, Bemtevi, as thou art a Bemtevi
and thou knowest not how to take leave....
O Bemtevi, even if far he be,
soon he shall return to me.

Though this is not the version of love I long for, there have been times when I had to remind myself how much I don't want it and how much I hate it when people try to make difficult things seem simple.

Like any woman who makes demands, Maria Gonçalves Cajada was almost entirely alone in her insistence that the world be fair and also that she be granted a just place in it. I appreciate deeply, almost as a kind of profession of faith, that there is an historical record, cited by Laura de Mello e Souza in *The Devil and the Land of the Holy Cross*, among others, of how a woman looked a priest in the eyes, then turned the other way to set three pieces of cheese fermented in her own vaginal fluid on a windowsill to feed the demons. It is a gesture with many layers of meanings which the centuries have distilled to a very lovely note ringing "I am."

When Maria wandered the countryside begging with her dear but inexperienced friend Domingas Fernandos, Maria told everybody Domingas was a saint and that touching or being touched by the nervous woman was a virtue. And she added, clever and practical, that it would cost you a certain number of cruzados to give such magic a try.

Another love spell from another of the accused that was recorded in the affidavits of the Visitation went like this:

> Souls, souls of the sea, of the land,
> three hanged, three dragged, three shot to death for love,
> all mine shall gather and into the heart
> and so shall enter and such tremor shall cause for love
> that none could rest nor be still
> save say yes to this wish.

I like this one better because this woman also told her clients that if the wish were granted doors would open and close, guitars would sound, stars would shoot. If not, asses would bray and dogs would bark. I like it that she leaves room for heartbreak and refusal. In the space between the poem and its answer, both lovers still have the freedom to make a choice. I like remembering that if I ever decide to change my life, it will still be my life to change.

It was an old friend who testified before the inquisitors and, trying to save herself, accused Maria of being a sorceress who nourished the devil. Two days earlier this friend had been denounced by a former lover who, to save his reputation, claimed to have been bewitched. The judges found his accusations as persuasive and compelling as hers, so they sentenced both women, plus many others.

It's a bad ending and I don't like it. I don't like that the moral becomes one about the treachery of women. I don't like that the only way to learn anything about Maria Gonçalves Cajada is to first learn that everyone called her by the nickname Arde-lhe-o-rabo, which translates as Butt-that-burns. That every index and parenthetical aside acknowledges the name by which the inquisitors, the torturers, and the cruelest of customers knew her, the one that came to her most likely as a side effect of sex work. I don't like that it was the name she was given because she was a woman who would tell nothing but the truth. I don't like that this is the way every story of radical friendship seems to end. But it only seems that way because of who has been allowed to write the stories. My dear friend read the first drafts and the last ones. She read the letters I sent and the ones I didn't. She read the ones I received too. I have confessed a lot here, but she is the one who showed me the whales and she has secrets of mine she will take to her grave.

So let's think instead for a moment about Domingas, who vanishes from the archives immediately after her journey with Maria is over. As far as we know anything could have happened to her. Though we cannot know what it was, we can surmise she was given something by her friend upon their parting. It might have been a rung of ladder or a plank of boat, a powder gathered from the back of some toad in the forest or an egg soaked in the magic of her pudenda. Maybe it made her invisible or invincible or rich enough to call herself free. Maybe it made it so she could find a way to go back home or to some new home or further along that mud-splattered road. Maybe it made it so she could become the person she always thought she had the right to be. If any part of what people said about her were true, I want it to be that Maria Gonçalves Cajada had this power to share and she did, that it touches the shores of our lives even now.

Medusa

Y ou begin a spell with an invocation like *Hear me* or *I beseech you* or *Oh friend* or *Listen*.

One of the things that can make a spell work is a description of a previous time the spell worked. The Anglo-Saxon *Æcerbot* to heal barren land, for example, begins by gathering parts of every kind of tree growing there except the hardwoods and parts of every known herb except the burrs, packing them with milk and honey into four blessed clods, and burying those clods at the corners of your acreage. A spell is most effective when you want something and can remember a time it already existed.

When you hear someone say Medusa was hideous with hair full of snakes, that is some xenophobic assholery by people who lived on the other shore of the Mediterranean Sea. When you hear she was a dangerous and vengeful witch, that means she was as measured in the congressional hearings on the subject of known-rapist Poseidon as any woman so subpoenaed always is. When you hear the corals of the Red Sea formed after Perseus set Medusa's head down for a moment on a bed of seaweed that had washed ashore, there were years I thought all the world was a Gorgon cave and I was already made of stone.

In a way that felt like corals being born into the sea, a person who loved me reached across to touch my wrist.

Though anthropological linguists caution against calling everything you don't understand magic, what doesn't feel possible when reading the Babylonian spells carved out from one of the oldest written languages? *Whether thou art a ghost that hath come from the earth, or a phantom of night that hath no couch ... or a ghost unburied, or a hag-demon, or a ghoul ... or a weeping woman that hath died with a babe at the breast ...* There is so little of what the people who invented writing wrote that every fragmented word of a busted stone tablet seems to be a spell. *Whatever thou be until thou art removed, until thou departest from the body of the man, thou shalt have no water to drink. Thou shalt not stretch forth thy hand.*

I was trying to understand the space between what seems possible and what can happen when the phenomenological linguist Maurice Merleau-Ponty said language itself is the spell. "There is no inner life," he wrote, "that is not a first attempt to relate to another person. In this ambiguous position, which has been forced on us because we have a body and history (both personally and collectively), we can never know complete rest."

Another word for the space between us is chiasm; neurobiologists use it to describe the anatomical region in the brain between the left and right hemispheres where neural fibers from the eyes interweave to form a single vision.

Medusa was brought into being by two chthonic monsters of the archaic world. Phorcys was the first merman and father of crabs. Ceto is the mother of whales.

I thought I was falling in love, but really I was so full of fury I didn't even know the half of it. My friend who believes in love and wants me to keep believing too read me H.D.'s *Notes on Thought and Vision* over the phone: "It is a closed sea-plant, jelly-fish or anemone. Into that over-mind thoughts pass and are like fish swimming under clear water.... There is, then, a set of super-feelings. These feelings extend out and about us; as the long floating tentacles of the jelly-fish reach out and about him." Her voice crossed a thousand miles to reach me in the cave at the bottom of my ear.

Maybe jellyfish were the spell I was looking for, she said, and that seemed possible too, because of how my mind and my body felt like tentacles longing to really be tentacles. Loricae, like caims, runes, and incantations, are litanies that make a circle. The word *lorica*, like the word *caim*, can be translated as *shield* or *armor*. I was such a lorica of busted coral reef.

Eventually the goddess Athena took possession of Medusa's head, which could still turn you to stone with nothing more than a glance across the chiasm, and she placed it on her shield.

"Whether speaking or listening, I project myself into the other person, I introduce him into my own self. Our conversation resembles a struggle between two athletes in a tug-of-war. The speaking 'I' abides in its body. Rather than imprisoning it, language is like a magic machine for transporting the 'I' into the other person's perspective," writes Merleau-Ponty.

In runes the letters are words but also the letters control the tenor of the spell, as in you must sing them, perhaps in a falsetto. Such a spell is about speaking out loud what was written in silence. The German root for *rune* means *whisper*. Derivatives appear in other languages as *secret, mystery, speech, to speak, to cut with a knife, poem*.

I speak to the gulls every morning when I pass them on my circle over the cliffs because I know I'm not going to leave my mind to live like a jellyfish in some starry pelagic zone where you can't find the beginning or end of your body. Except when I have and except when I do.

Merleau-Ponty urges us to keep trying to listen and trying to say what we mean. Stay with it long enough, he reassures, and you will come to understand "human languages are informed not only by the structure of the human body and the human community, but by the evocative shapes and patterns of the more-than-human terrain."

When Perseus beheaded Medusa, the Pegasus she had been carrying flew forth from her body and passed through the whole sky in orbiting astonishment at how far this blue world goes. Her offspring, winged and airy and free, gazed upon weary and trembling Atlas, then, in Pegasus's only recorded act of magic, turned the giant to stone. Which is one way to explain how it is I am still here, trying to understand the meanings and the possibilities inherent in every word that passes between us.

Angéle de la Barthe

Thomas Aquinas wondered if our atmosphere was a punishment for demons. He concluded no, but also wondered if demons could experience sorrow. He concluded no, but wondered if the will of the demon was obstinate in evil. He concluded not really, but wondered if they, being coagulated creatures of air, could produce spawn by copulating with witches. He concluded no, but what if they disguised themselves as women to steal the seed of men?

This must be how Angéle de la Barthe, a well-known woman of property and means in Aquinas's Toulouse came to be a mother at age fifty-two. (Or was it sixty-four? Accounts vary ...) Wolf-headed, serpent-tailed, her child, it was said, fed on the fresh corpses of infants for two years, before he ran away in the night.

Or so she said after the inquisitor Hugo de Beniols tortured her and threatened to burn her alive if she did not confess.

Or perhaps she said. In 1275, congress with demons was not yet listed as a crime. And there are no transcripts of her trial, though there is no shortage of them from other trials in that same year. So serious historians consider the fifteenth-century chronicle of her so-called life to be specious and apocryphal, imperfect to the point of meaninglessness.

Angéle de la Barthe was of the gnostic sect of Cathars, so like Aquinas, the devoted Catholic, she would have believed the air was on invisible fire with an aether of demons snatching at souls as they glimmered past. Unlike Catholics, as a Cathar she would have believed in a dualist philosophy of a good god and an evil god who were equally powerful and held each other in balance.

Also, she was wealthy. She owned her own property and thus wielded some degree of influence in the city of Toulouse, which was a stronghold of those who would resist the authority of the Church. They abandoned baptisms there, for example, because Cathars thought it absurd that you had to buy the holy water from a traveling priest when water is material and the spirit is immaterial.

Whenever a Cathar mother and father made a new baby, a body that would cage another soul for a lifetime, they felt they had been very weak and were very sorry. This strikes me as easily miserable as anything the Catholics believed, but the part where gender was of no consequence to them because bodies were of no consequence to them is appealing.

But to the inquisitors a woman in authority was confusing and created a sense of disorder—you might call it a feeling of bedevilment—among those friars loyal to the papacy who witnessed it. Or perhaps I am being specious and apocryphal.

I keep remembering that boyfriend I once had who was so excited when we stumbled on Aquinas's grave in Toulouse. Who knew, we said to each other, that Toulouse had once been at the center of so much philosophical inquiry and intrigue? Not me, whose Catholic education was designed to inculcate a spirit of obedience and discipline. And not him, who had been raised to inherit the earth. He went on and on about how Aquinas was his favorite philosopher, the one who proved the existence of God. It seemed to me Aquinas must have been the only philosopher that boyfriend of mine had ever read and that what had been proved was nothing.

Having read the Summa Theologica the summer before, just to prove I was smart, it was tempting to spit on the grave of yet another man pretending to know so much. But it was important to me then to be nice, so I waited until we got home to break up. He called me a bitch, naturally, and said I didn't know how to love and I was going to die alone. It took a certain amount of willpower not to laugh right into his teary face. Perhaps he deserved it, but he was so sad to be this mean. He was under the impression he loved me and also that he knew anything about me.

Thomas Aquinas wondered what knowledge was and who might have what portion of it. He proposed, "The proper knowledge of the angels is twofold; namely morning and evening. But the demons have no morning knowledge."

Goodness as a form of morning knowledge is a beautiful idea, but let's not forget Aquinas also said children resulting from demonic congress, children like the one Angéle de la Barthe was tortured into admitting she had, were "icy creatures that rode the winds and assailed the bodies and minds of their human prey."

What I was thinking, but didn't say, to that ex of mine was that I didn't particularly care if I ever loved again. That I was looking for something more than this knotted cord of the erotic, something that would really be worth the shortness of my time and the limitations of my attention.

I have tried to be Catholic and tried to be Cathar. I have tried to be worthy of the air I breathe. I made myself miserable many times over trying to embody the ascetic opposite of whatever it was I thought I wanted.

Aquinas said perfection is when a thing is perfect in itself or when it perfectly serves its purpose. Good luck figuring out when or if that might ever be you.

There has been much disagreement about what constitutes even a perfect number. Passionate advocates can be found throughout the Middle Ages for 3, 7, and 10. Lately the mathematicians are partial to numbers that equal the sum of their divisors that are smaller than themselves. 6, for example, = 1 + 2 + 3. Euclid identified four of these: 6, 28, 496, and 8128. But doesn't it seem like there should be a perfect number of perfect numbers? After two thousand years of recorded investigations, it is still unknown whether the number of perfect numbers is infinite or even whether a perfect number can be odd.

In physics there is the "perfectly plastic," "perfectly rigid," "perfectly fluid," "perfectly black," and the "crystal." None of these can be found in nature; they are merely extreme ideals nature might be understood to approach. Perfection is a concept designed to make it possible to think beyond what we already know.

On the list of known paradoxes you can find this one: the greatest perfection is imperfection, because it so perfectly attains the limits of its own ideal.

Before Thomas Aquinas there was Saint Gregory, who said that perfection will only be realized after the fulfillment of history.

That guy, the old story goes, once heard the deathbed confession of a monk in his order who had stolen three gold pieces. Gregory cast every friend the sick man had out of the room so the thief would die alone. Then threw the failed body on a manure pile and the three coins after him, saying he should take the gold with him to perdition. There is no reason, the saint thought, that God's punishments should not begin on earth.

But perhaps this account is also specious and apocryphal.

If I were Angéle de la Barthe I would have confessed to whatever bullshit they wanted to hear too. And when they burned me after all, for what I said, instead of what I didn't say, I guess, like most of the people in this situation on a pyre, I wouldn't bother with pleas or curses either.

Like some chronicler out of the fifteenth century, I have been asking dead people to help me understand what my life is for. I imagine how this woman would have watched the sun rising beyond the crowd, noticing how nice it feels when a beam of morning light warms the skin of your shoulder like the hand of a person you desire or a very fine silk fabric that proves itself worth its cost when you feel the thrill of how it slips down your arm, almost but not quite, as if it was never meant to be there in the first place.

If you want to give up everything, your life in pursuit of someone else's ideas of perfection seems like a good place to start.

Bloodroot

When we set out to hunt jewelweed, I had Asclepius on my mind. Asclepius, who gave humans both medicine and magic in the form of a bag of herbs. He was instructed in the art of medicine by the centaur Chiron, who raised him after his pregnant mother was killed by the god Apollo for her infidelity. He was lifted, newborn, from the ashes of her funeral pyre. Later, he rendered some now-forgotten kindness to a snake, who licked his ears clean in return and then whispered into them all its secret knowledge. In this way he became a healer who could bring people back from the brink and beyond.

Every time we start over I think I'll write the field guide to the beautiful weeds on the new acreage. There was the ironweed and wingstem farm that was lush and relentless. Then there was the chicory and thistle farm where I was as much a terrible fire season of a drought as the pasture was. Both farms were the farms where I became more and more out of practice talking. And, as the years went by, made my way into the inconvenience of town less and less.

Evermore, my voice sounded strange outside my head. After a while the field guides became conversations with and then love letters to the plants, who felt like the only things I knew how to know. There came a time when I realized what I was calling "ecofeminist botanical mysticism" is a phenomenon that psychiatrists call by other, more usefully descriptive names. I was, as they say, trying to keep a troubling sense of unreality at bay.

On the way to the creek to fill my bag with herbs, we had a fight about the new front yard. About what it meant to live in a neighborhood now and not an island of our own acreage. About what constitutes a weed. About what manners are and friendliness is. We were having a fight about whether we were willing to keep having fights.

When I tore out the new street-facing hillside of plants you might call wildflowers or you might call weeds, I was trying something new. I was living without explanation or compromise or apology. The hill was a surprise garden of harebells, anemone, and wild mustard. Or it was a weedy entanglement of poison ivy. It was both, of course, but another name for my experiment was "I only believe in my version of reality." The results of this field research: he was pissed and I was pissed.

With Asclepius on my mind, I was hoping we'd find jewelweed to rub on the poison ivy rash covering my neck and arms and face. My neck? My face? I was trying not to freak out, because that makes it worse, of course. But I kept touching my cheek and then taking a deep breath and then touching my cheek again anyway. It was the kind of rash that makes you wonder if you aren't being punished for a terrible mistake. But also it seemed like an invitation to make more mistakes, because when it's this bad, how much more do you have to lose?

There are as many rumors of remedies for poison ivy as there are wishes things could be different. You can make a salve of heavily salted milk or sour milk beaten until it is thick. You can make a salve of cow slobber. You can make one of nightshade berries mixed with sweet cream. You can put ironweed roots in an iron pot so they stand upright and cook them to make a liquid for washing the rash. You can wash the rash in apple vinegar. You can carry a pocketful of rifle cartridges to prevent or cure the poisoning.

I came to regret tearing out that bed. The roots of harebells form a staircase into hell. Anemones are the last breath of one of Aphrodite's undying loves. Wild mustard can be turned into a poultice to ease the wheeze of a chest cold. Columbine is useful for birth control and also can give you the courage of an eagle. And of course everything, even the weed-choked or withering or chaotic tangled things, are pretty if you can look at them from the right angle. That everything-at-once-ness is the beauty of being alive—I was wrong to hoe up that bed, but also I was right. And anyway, all of it came back with vigor the next year and the one after that.

In a fight between people who have been married for fifteen years many things that are not part of the story are nevertheless part of it. For example, it is and is not part of the story that right after we moved he filed a police report about the neighbor whose dog was always barking. It is and is not part of the story that the dog didn't bother me at all and I was deeply embarrassed to be roped into such a conflict by virtue of nothing more than being his wife and having my name beside his on the deed. It is and is not part of the story that we were new in town and I just wanted to bend to what was normal in the neighborhood for a while. It was the summer we didn't get a divorce, but moved instead from the farm to a cottage in town because I said I was going with or without him. It is and is not part of the story that he missed the deep isolation of the woods where he had spent his whole life. It is and is not part of the story that if I let myself think about how sorry I was for him and what it was like for him to give up so much, my stomach would ache like a hole in the earth where someone just dug out all its mayapple.

In the beginning, everything I knew about the green world I learned from him. During the leanest years of his childhood he poached wild ginseng and black cohosh off government land for small handfuls of cash from an old herbalist living in a trailer near Bear Creek who then sold remedies to homeopaths up in the city where I was learning a whole different brand of resourcefulness. But after enough years together, there came a day when I knew everything about plants that he did, and then there came a day after when I knew more than he did. On the day that happened we didn't notice. We didn't notice for a long time.

All of the accounts of Chiron make a great deal of how he was different from all the other centaurs — his front legs were human rather than equine, he was born of a nymph and a Titan. A real centaur has four equine legs. A real centaur is born of the union between the sun and a rain cloud. Real centaurs are the stampede of storm. Real or not, all of the centaurs know how to read the stars and how to interpret the dew pearling on the leaves. If you really want to know how to live, you can start with Asclepius, but sooner or later you will have to go directly to those wild, dangerous, beautiful horses.

To learn all of the stories and all of the magic, the great folklorist Zora Neale Hurston would pretend to be in love or pretend not to be. She pretended to be a logger and a priestess and that she was unambiguously eager to be Franz Boas's favorite student. She drank and danced and fasted and crept through dense woods. Though most of the magic involving poison ivy is about how you can use other plants to cure it, poison ivy has its uses as an agent too. Hurston recorded one spell that involves putting the dried crushed leaves, along with some other herbs, into a little sachet you slip under the pillow of a man who has wronged you to ruin his peace and his dreams.

I've heard quite a few stories about fearless, always-in-trouble kids on the playground, the ones who have come from someplace beyond the limits of a prim schoolteacher's imagination, proving they were not to be trifled with by plucking a leaf of three and eating it before all of the aghast children buttoned so neatly into their future college degrees. There's pretty good evidence from double-blind studies tucked away in the journals of modern medicine that this is, in fact, an effective way to make yourself immune to the urushiol in the leaves over time. There's pretty good evidence in double-blind studies that whatever you think you might know about how things work, you should not assume you really know.

Before I covered myself in calamine lotion, I wanted to see if the rumors about jewelweed might also be true. A plant with watery, succulent stems, the antidote is to crush the leaves in your hands and then rub your skin vigorously with the released juices. It often grows interlaced with poison ivy, which herbalists say is always the way—poison loves its antidote. Like a marriage.

There was a time when the puzzle of our disagreements interested me so deeply it was its own form of love. He was 350 acres of pasturelands, and *soo cow, soo* in the hot sun. He was this holler of a grandfather's abandoned cabin and that sweet spring of a great-uncle's old claim. I was dandelion-busted concrete and cars backfiring, *Was that a gunshot?* I used to like it when someone wrecked what I thought I knew to be true. It made me feel like living was a form of floating. It was reassuring to live inside such constant proof of my one axiom that there is no certain knowing.

Then I changed. I was tired of feeling like my life was to be spent endlessly tangled up in my opposite. I was tired of dithering and hand-wringing and the dizziness of shifting my mind from this view to that one and back again. I could tell the stories of all the little fights, but they are so inconsequential and boring. Why did these insignificant things hurt my feelings so much? I felt like I was living inside the body of a spooked deer that would never stop running. I'd had a vision for a different sort of hillside — the too-tall Jerusalem artichoke would be at the back, the harebells would be bunched next to daisies and a domestic ornamental variety of columbine with blossoms large enough to hold the eye. The anemones could have the flat strip at the bottom and spill into the road. Every plant would be a check against some other plant's inclination to clamor and scraggle. I had a vision where there would be a kind of geometry that would hold still long enough to be made into sense.

And then I understood it was all very simple. I wanted a garden and since a garden is about containing chaos inside of order, I was willing to tear out a hillside of wildflowers, then plant the exact same species back to have it. I started to see that whatever else happened, I was also the antidote to myself.

Jewelweed has other names, like lady's-eardrop and lady's slipper, which are perfect descriptors of the little resting butterflies of its orange flowers among those deep green leaves. For some reason it is also called touch-me-not. I can see no reason for that name, since what we do is crush that plant between our palms, then smear the ichor on what ails. For all its wrongness, touch-me-not is my favorite name for this plant and I covered myself in it.

When he filed the report about the dog, people at the precinct, he said, were sympathetic. Apparently they agreed the noise would make them nuts too. And later the neighbor was really apologetic. They shook hands. The house was quiet for days and days, then month after month. He became cheerful now that he could sleep again. He planted strawberries in some of the barren places in the yard while humming himself an old song about a boy with a gun and good hunting dog.

We went through the jewelweed on the banks and beyond to the ridge where blackberries tumble themselves down the thin soil of the piney bluffs. We ate them as we rested at the overlook, watching the water run its clear trickle across the bed of quartz below. The trees dappled golden and spackled their shade as he pointed to some heart-shaped leaves and said, "Oh, bloodroot." This is one of the plants he used to dig for money—when you pulverize the root it secretes a disinfectant as orange and chilly as iodine. The Sanguinarine nurses pour from a bottle with an intimidating label while you sit in the chill white of the examination room has been sitting here in the loam of these Ozark woods the whole time.

Sometimes I wonder if I ever would have discovered forests or plants, Chiron or spells, if it hadn't been for him and how he took me to them. He was so charmed on that first hike when I looked around at the river bottoms tangled up in wild woody grape vines and said, thinking of that city arboretum at the center of my childhood, "I didn't know nature was so messy." Would I know if he hadn't shown me that you're never really lost? When you get tired of feeling lost, he says, just go down into a holler and follow it, either way, until you come to water, and you will come to water because hollers are made by rain. When you come to water, follow it, either way, until you come to a bridge, and you will come to a bridge because sooner or later people want something on the other side. And now I am the one to tell him that sooner or later, on either side, jewelweed will be there, because it's one of those plants that's like poison ivy. No matter how much you spray or mow or weed or pull, it survives and comes back. It's one of those plants that will be with us until the end of the world.

I forget sometimes that there were many years when there was nothing but us and the perfect silence of our acres and I was happy for a great many of them. I changed, but I haven't stopped loving the brown silence of a mushroom blooming one ear after another along a crash of limb.

Clumps of soil are sticking to his palm as he holds up the orange tuber of a bloodroot. "Anybody have any cuts?" he asks. But no, I just have this rash. He insists, "Let's do it anyway." So I hold out my hand and he busts the root in half to smear some of that bright red ooze on my wrist. He's shown me bloodroot before, but never broken out the secret elixir it keeps below the dirt. I wonder if it really is that these plants, his and mine, are helping, or if it's just that time, that very good medicine, is passing. Whatever it is, I feel a little better. And when I ask him, he says he feels better too.

The Long Lost Friend

A well-laid hex can last a long time. Pow-Wows or, Long Lost Friend: A Collection of Mysterious and Invaluable Arts and Remedies, for Man As Well As Animals, with Many Proofs of Their Virtue and Efficacy in Healing Diseases, Etc., was an Americanized English translation of a very old book of spells and home remedies. From the German tradition of braucherei, it was translated as "pow-wow," an appropriation in keeping with the many other violences European immigrants would commit against Algonquin and other indigenous peoples.

In this book, the line between magic and folk wisdom is not a line, but a gauzy billowing. There are spells to make molasses and beer, recipes for eye-water, words to protect a traveler on a journey, remedies for burns and colic. To prevent a wicked or malicious person from doing you an injury, you should recite the following: "Dullix, ix, ux. Yea you can't come over Pontio, Pontio is above Pilato." To cure epilepsy, take a turtle dove, cut its throat, and let the person afflicted with epilepsy drink the blood. For the spell "To Prevent Gun-Barrels from Rusting," you will need an ounce of bear's fat, half an ounce of badger's grease, half an ounce of snake's fat, one ounce of almond oil, and a quarter of an ounce of pulverized indigo.

To hear John Blymire tell it, the hex Nelson Rehmeyer put on him had lasted his whole life, from the moment he was born.

To hear Nelson Rehmeyer tell it, Who is John Blymire and why would I curse a man I don't know, or anybody at all?

We used to live not so very far from the place where John Blymire murdered Nelson Rehmeyer. A state away, but still inside the orbit of all those old hex signs on the barns and whispers of this or that granny woman and what folks remember of how she used to heal. Our defunct dairy farm straddled a stretch of Sunday Creek and in that place my husband and I liked to sit on the back porch making plans for the crumble-down barn on our stretch of the banks. We thought it would be idyllically pastoral to hang one of the old charm signs over the hayloft. My favorite was the good-luck distelfink which is a stylized bird with a red feather coming out of the top of his eye that makes you think of quail. There is a curving fretwork of blue feathers down his neck like an echo of fish. The wings are a yellow plumage of jagged lightning folded close against the body. The distelfink often perches atop a tulip that means faith but opens out petals like a kiss.

Like most everyone else in those coal-boom turned depopulated and opioid-addled towns known as Little Cities of the Black Diamond, we found it hard to justify the expense of barn paint when we were being so carefully, anxiously strategic about groceries and gas. The foundation was leaking and the furnace had a troublesome rattle that echoed through the silent winter.

A local conservation group hired my husband for minimum wage to be an assistant to the water-quality specialist, because he knew something about wildlife biology and something about lab work, and because once in another watershed another lifetime ago he lost the Ozark farm of his childhood to the lead mines that owned the underground rights beneath his family's farm and sunk the water table during a bad drought summer. There was a spring next to the foundation of his great-grandfather's cabin that burbled up a little creek where the cows drank. That summer the water ran yellow and then it didn't run at all.

Sometimes our stretch of Sunday Creek ran gray and turbid like smoke and we did not know why, despite repeated phone calls to Buckingham Coal who still had a dig upstream. In Truetown, nine miles downstream of us the creek had long since turned orange and stank of rotten eggs because of a collapsed nineteenth-century mine. Gob piles of coal too poor to burn lined the creek banks in a tarry mess of barren sludge weeping acid for a hundred years now.

Old-timers say you can dunk your kid in the waters of that acid mine drainage, holding on tight to her ankles, to cure her of lice. It's the kind of spell you can find in Long Lost Friend beside suggestions for stinging nettles, which are "Good for Banishing Fears and Fancies, and to Cause Fish to Collect." The book promises, "Whenever you hold this weed in your hand together with Millifolia, you are safe from all fears and fancies that frequently deceive men." It goes on to say, more practically, "If you mix it with a decoction of hemlock, and rub your hands with it, and put the rest in water that contains fish, you will find the fish to collect around your hands." I read this to my husband on a day when he came home sweaty and broke-down tired after dragging a 150 lb. generator through a mile of brush to send voltage through their nets to shock the fish. Momentarily stunned, the creatures bob to the surface, where the scientists record their paltry numbers and the distressing absence of certain key indicator species. Before long they flicker back to life and disappear beneath the murk once more. If only he had known it could be so much easier, he says, stretching his sore arms out behind his back.

Here is a remedy to be applied when anyone is sick. "Let the sick person, without having converse with anyone, put water in a bottle before sunrise, close it up tight, and put it immediately in some box or chest. Lock it up and stop up the keyhole; the key must be carried in one of the pockets for three days, as nobody dare have it except the person who puts the bottle with water in the chest or box." There are no instructions about what to do at the end of three days. Drink the water? Pour it down the drain? Forget you ever put it in that box in the first place?

I wonder how clear the water was running or how long it had been left in its dark box when John Blymire went to see Nellie Noll, who everyone called The River Witch. According to the newspaper reports from that terrible summer in 1928, it was the river witch who told him he needed a lock of Nelson Rehmeyer's hair and a copy of his spell book to burn in order to lift the curse of his hard life. First he scouted out the Rehmeyer place by pretending he was a hungry hobo. Rehmeyer gave him lodging that night and fed him breakfast in the morning. He poured him coffee and passed the syrup. Blymire came back the next night with two teenage accomplices, fourteen-year-old John Curry and eighteen-year-old Wilbert Hess.

There is a remedy you can use when anyone is falling away, and which, the book swears, has cured many persons. "Let the person in perfect soberness and without having conversed with anyone, catch rain in his pot, before sunrise; boil an egg in this; bore three small holes in this egg with a needle, and carry it to an ant hill made by big ants; and that person will feel relieved as soon as the egg is devoured."

Where we lived there was no talk of river witches or Nellie Noll. There was only Mountain Mary and her legendary goodness. With her hands alone, the old-timers said, she could heal you. But all you can find now of Mountain Mary is her name. It's on a forest here, a wet-weather ditch there. There are the last few logs of this or that abandoned cabin in the way-back woods people say must have once been hers.

Those who know well the spells in *Long Lost Friend* say she would have saved you with these words from Ezekiel:

> And when I passed by thee and saw thee polluted in thine own blood, I said unto thee when thou wast in thy blood, Live; yea, I said unto thee when thou wast in thy blood, Live.

They say she was something powerful good in the midst of these terrible hard hills, they say she walks them sometimes still like a sweet wind looking to brush past your hair and make you all right.

There is a mist every morning that fills up the hollers so thick you can hardly see, and then there comes a moment each day when you crest a high ridge and see the sun all of a sudden fully risen. You can look down the valleys to the barns, some red, most gray with age and neglect, a few very fine ones decorated by a large painted quilt square or one of the many hex signs. A red horse head in silhouette protects animals from disease and the barn from lightning. A maple leaf brings contentment, oak leaves are for strength. Often the two symbols interweave in a sunburst of fortitude and happiness. Raindrops are a call-down promise of fertility for the soil and the family.

On other days there is that other haze, the one still smoking out of the earth, ever since 1884 when miners in New Straitsville had been striking hard against the poverty, the exploitation, and the dangerous working conditions. When the owners brought in scabs, the miners slipped into the coal seams and started a fire. By the time anyone who might have stopped it realized what was happening, the underground was blazing and a hundred years later it's still burning, smoke still escaping through sinkholes to the surface every now and again. The mixture of defiance and righteous indignation cutting against the unforeseen consequences of foolhardy violence seems sometimes like the truest story this place knows how to tell about itself.

That was an old mining disaster, but there keep on being new ones. Every time an old dig collapses, a new fountain of sludgy poison springs out of the ground. The Upper Big Branch Mine disaster was in 2010 and twenty-nine people died digging coal out from beneath a West Virginia mountain. It still hangs heavy on the minds of these Little Cities.

The spell to prevent conflagration is a long and complicated affair involving a black chicken, a scrap of shirt worn by a chaste virgin and cut off according to her own terms, an egg laid on a Thursday, wax, pots, and various days of burying things beneath the threshold. Another method of stopping fire is to say these words:

> Our dear Sarah journeyed through the land,
> having a fiery hot brand in her hand.
> The fiery brand heats, the fiery brand sweats.
> Fiery brand, stop your beat.
> Fiery brand, stop your sweat.

Long Lost Friend is the kind of book where "beat" is perhaps a typo and should read "heat" or perhaps is exactly what the author intended. Among the dozen ways to stop bleeding, one is to say these words:

> I walk through a green forest;
> There I find three wells, cool and cold;
> The first is called courage,
> The second is called good,
> And the third is called stop the blood.

I have gone and will go to many public hearings. I know the spell "To Gain a Lawful Suit." I know you take large leaves of sage and write the names of the twelve apostles on them, then put these in your shoes before entering the courthouse. Nevertheless, our little town and all of our neighboring towns took "donations" of fresh coal ash the companies were otherwise required by law to dispose of as hazardous waste. To save money they used the flakes instead of salt on the roads in the winter. So with spring thaws new coal ash ran off the sides of roads directly into the creeks and we didn't even have to wait for some new disaster to turn another spring orange.

Nevertheless, treatment plans for the worst acid mine drainage sites were proposed. One city council voted the plan down because the acid neutralized the wastewater they dumped directly into the creek, as they had no sewage system. Another reason was that the passive treatment ponds full of water reeds and other plants that would filter the toxins through their roots would not look as sightly as a smooth mowed lawn. Hanging heavy in the air of so many meetings was the conviction you couldn't trust scientists and you couldn't trust conservationists and you couldn't trust people with nothing more to show for themselves than pride in all their degrees and accomplishments come to tell folks what to do.

During these public hearings mountaintops were removed. The earth began to shake as fracking destabilized the balance of bedrock and shale beneath our water table. We asked ourselves if orange water weren't the least of our worries and we knew the answer was simply that we had too many worries.

What happened to Nelson Rehmeyer is that no spell book could be found anywhere in his house or on his property. So the two men and the fourteen-year-old boy bludgeoned him, bound him to a chair, and set him on fire while he was still breathing. Despite being doused in kerosene, the body did not completely burn, which investigators said was one of the truly horrific things they'd ever seen.

What happened to Nelson Rehmeyer is that he gave food and shelter to the people who would slaughter him, to people who did not know how to know a blessing when the plate was handed to them.

What happened is this. When an old woman dies, she is dead, her cabin crumbles to the ground, and she's not around anymore to put her hand on your cheek and tell you it's going to be all right.

When you light an old man on fire, whether he be some old witch or the spirit of a mountain or just a kind and generous bachelor, now he is dead too. There is nothing that is going to change that.

Long Lost Friend is a broken book. A support beam cracked, the roof collapsed, the water poured in or the fire did, the tailings and the ash everywhere. Now no one dares drink from the poison of those pages. It has spells to make divining rods, spells to lift a curse, spells for mending. I wish I believed it could do us any good.

> To Mend Broken Glass: Take common cheese and wash it well, unslaked lime and the white of eggs, rub all these well together until it becomes one mass, and then use it. If it is made right, it will certainly hold.

The Eye of the Hagstone

The Black River burbles up from caves beneath the Ozark Mountains. Standing in its shallows, watching small fry dash and school just beyond the ripples of my steps, I found a rock the size of my palm with a large hole through the center like a stone monocle. My husband, out to his waist in the water, still mud-caked from belly-crawling a way through a spring-formed cave that morning said, "Oh wow, that's a really good hagstone." If you look through a hole in a stone, he added, you can see beyond the veil, through a glamour, into a wretched heart.

I looked, expecting to see nothing, but in fact the light was entirely changed, every sparkle on the water crystallized and magnified, the air itself glowed; even Brian, smiling at arm's length, seemed to radiate.

Hagstones are abundant in landscapes with karst topographies where limestone or dolomite or gypsum bedrock is easily honeycombed by natural springs. In some places they are called adderstones or hexstones, Odin stones or chicken gods. They are used to bind evil spirits, bless the water, protect livestock. They can help you see what is real.

Even though I was the one writing the book on witches, when I held up this strangely shaped rock I had no idea what a hagstone was. It's often this way with us — I follow him into the cave, he follows me out. We got married too young, we sometimes say when blending in among the upper-class intelligentsia we have tried to become. But as the years pass we're learning how utterly we belong, if anywhere, to this isolated place where the ground is all secret caverns beneath our feet and the water is delicious because it passes through them on the way down and again on the way back up.

Out here it's taken by many as an axiomatic truth that people never change and a grudge is something you take to your grave. Perhaps that's why Isobel Gowdie, the Scottish witch put on trial in 1662, is the one who has always felt closest to me. Or perhaps because she came from a place some of my ancestors would have called home. Or because she was a flyter, a flinger of insults as a literary art form, which was a common practice among professional storytellers in her time and place, and lately feels like my own most-preferred genre. The court records do not include any examples of her flytes — by the time she had submitted to give her confession she was long past the balance between risk and restraint, the artful attention to sound and syntax that characterize the form. Instead she devoted that public performance almost entirely to asserting a violent and otherworldly power as she threatened, cursed, and hexed the men in the room. You can almost see her spit as you read the dozen and more names of neighbors she says she pierced with fairy arrows as she flew through the sky like a straw in a whirlwind.

Some of the great flytes that survived from her age into ours and that she might have borrowed from in happier times when performing at the market for a laughing and gasping crowd include:

In the Book of the Dun Cow, Emer won the Ulster Women's War-of-Words when she derided her rivals that "Your fine heroes are not worth a stalk of grass ... they are like the scum and the leavings."

In the Elder Edda Hrimgerdr told Atli "you would neigh if your balls weren't cut off," and Atli answered that he was a stallion and if he came ashore she would lower her tail.

Scottish court records include a transcription of the flyte between Marion Ray and Henry Anderson not so many years apart or towns away from Gowdie. "Slobbering Henry," Marion Ray said, "if you were worthy to fuck your wife yourself, you wouldn't let others fuck her." Henry's wife Agnes Anderson jumped into the fray to assert that Marion was a homewrecker and a whore.

Isobel Gowdie was likely a real witch, if by "witch" you mean a shamanic specialist operating at the social margins and employing syncretized folk traditions that incorporated elements of an ancient agrarian cult with the medieval Catholicism that had been forced on her people by English colonization. This was the definition I learned from the eminent historian Emma Wilby in *The Visions of Isobel Gowdie*, but a simpler way to say it is "cunning woman." To heal a sick child, she said in her confession, she diverted the sickness into a dog by "shakis the belt abow the fyre, [*damaged—words missing*] down to the ground, till a dowg or a catt goe ower it." A common charm among Scottish cunning women, found as often in poems and letters that alluded to these widespread folk healers as it is in the transcripted words of tortured women on trial for witchcraft. Isobel's trial for such acts was likely a consequence of the landed gentry's hardening commitment to a rigid Calvinism, which provided the lairds with theological justifications for maintaining strong personal holds over the estates to which families like Isobel's were tied as tenant farmers.

This transition in customs was abrupt—before, women were allowed to flyte in the streets for the delight and amusement of their neighbors; suddenly, this became cursing, an act of malfeasance. Before, a trial in such a small, rural community was just one more occasion to tell one of your very good stories with only the risk of a modest fine for such sorcery; now a trial was the place where diplomatic displays of fealty to a colonial order were enacted with nooses and fire. Before, you could gather with friends and family and complain about how the landlord just raised the rent again so how are you supposed to live. After, you were a dangerous coven who wished to see him and all his heirs dead.

To think about witches is to think about shifting perspectives. A spell or an amulet or a talisman is sometimes helpful in letting a person imagine a different world is possible. Though I personally do not believe the spells, hexes, fairies, or transmogrification of people into animals that Gowdie describes in her confessions are possible, I am committed to believing women.

Phenomenologists use the term "homeworld" to describe the kind of lived experiences and epistemological assumptions that shape a person into knowing what they know and knowing it in the way they know. My homeworld, for example, bears many features of the oppressive Catholicism I was raised in and many other landmarks shaped by how I said no to that faith and to the elders pushing it on me. It is a world perched on pillars of defiance and guilt, martyrs and monsters. When I meet a witch I try to find a passage from the world I understand into the one they do. Sometimes, when I'm looking through these hagstones, I get caught between.

How different is it for Isobel Gowdie to have believed, as she confessed she did, that "I wes in the downie hillis, and got meat ther from the qwein of the fearrie" than for my relations to pray a queen of saints will lead me home from the pagan path I seem to be on? When she described the exhilaration of flying over the countryside to the sea and back in the company of the devil and her coven, saying they were "thes strawes in whirlwind"—well, haven't I known well how erotic it can be to float and spin and fling myself beyond the limits of all reason?

For years I thought I was just a dumb girl who didn't get it—"it" being *The Critique of Pure Reason*, the collected poems of John Donne, the whistle from across the street, why a man would shout "bitch" from the window of his car into the ear of a passing stranger, the blood pouring down my legs as I clung to my seizing belly. How careful I once was to remain polite and respectful when the doctor answered my question about what he'd just asked a nurse to inject me with by muttering, "You read too much," before he went back to yanking my placenta out by the umbilical cord. Even now it feels as perilous as a flyte to suggest the scientific method is just one more socially constructed epistemological system of communal faith in a particular kind of truth, no more valid than a spell. Such a risk to dare assert the lead tailings oozing through the soil where we lay our picnic blankets, the crop-dusting biplane overhead, the keening I feel for the nearly extinct tinytim earthfruits and pondberries and grotto sculpins and yellow mud turtle, all this is predicated on that moment when René Descartes imagined he could, like a god, invent a whole world out of nothing but the thought "I think, therefore I am."

Am I starting to believe Gowdie when she says "all the witches yet that are untaken haw their owin poweris and our poweris which we haid"? I asked the critical theorists, who cast the rune stones I know how to read, and Zaid Ahmad answered that he too wants to find ways for all of us to know each other. In his essay comparing homeworlds, he recounts how it was in roughly the same period, but on the other side of the Mediterranean Sea, that Ibn-Khaldūn, like Descartes, tried to figure out what would allow a person to believe their own senses. He concluded you are alive when you can wonder how it feels to some other being to feel alive. Ibn-Khaldūn's homeworld is based on *fikr*, unlike Descartes's, which is built on the *cogito*. Fikr: by asking the stones how it feels to be them, Ibn-Khaldūn heard in his question the very nature of his own being.

Isobel Gowdie, it seems, knew she was alive by how she was fighting. She cursed Harry Forbes, the man who first accused and then interrogated her, reciting three times the refrain: "He is lyeing in his bed and he is lyeing seik and sore, let him lye intill his bed, two monethis days more." These confessions of maleficium, if they are evidence of anything, prove perhaps her real desire to give certain men what she thought they deserved.

For a long time I couldn't understand Brian and I couldn't understand myself. Anger raised the veil. I cursed him with a packed bag in my hand. I said terrible things that made us really separate, that made it easy to see myself as separate in a way that women, so often known only as wives and mothers, have to fight to know. Once I understood myself alone, I understood him, maybe for the first time. It felt possible after that to know other people too.

Hagstones emerge from boundary sites like caves and are powerful for being portholes born of portholes. In the hagstone's eye we can see Isobel Gowdie for the bard that she was. Her confessions employ "powerful and vivid verbs, often in multiples: the Devil was 'beating and scurgeing'; elf bulls were 'crowtting and skrylling'; and the elf boys were 'whytting and dighting.'" In the eye of the hagstone we see that so-familiar figure of the slumlord in the form of John Hay, the Laird of Park, trying to distract from and forestall his inevitable bankruptcy by crying witchcraft in the direction of anyone who grumbled at the sight of his face. We see Harry Forbes, the insolvent minister about to lose his congregation to changing theological tides and further undermined by credible rumors that he had an adulterous relationship with a servant. The trial cannot hold its glamour and we see this communion of judges, all deranged with fear they might lose a kind of power no one should have in the first place, pointing in the direction of persons they cannot, will not, see at all.

My hagstone emerged from the Eminence dolomite, formed by a chemical solution in carbonate rock. Water moving through the cave was charged into a weak carbonic acid that never filtered back to a neutral pH. I have always preferred spells for dreams and visions to love spells. Though I am charmed by the love spell's promise of human connection, I want something more powerful than another tepid rom-com. Charles Leland recorded a spell to activate hagstones in his nineteenth-century survey of European agrarian shamanic practices, *Etruscan Roman Remains*, which I have whispered into the ear of my stone:

> In the name of great Saint Peter
> And for Saint Blausius's sake,
> By this stone I fain would see,
> What form the spirits take.

In that year when I felt myself separating I was desperate for a vision. But I couldn't tell in what direction of separation or desperation I was headed. It seemed almost funny to buy a volume called *On Lies, Secrets, and Silence* at the used bookstore. Though it was no joke I was hoping someone—maybe a philosopher or feminist theorist, a flyter or a witch—would give me permission to have the affair or go insane or disappear into a mysticism I didn't really believe in.

Instead there was Adrienne Rich, already dog-eared and underlined in faint pencil, insisting I had to figure out how I was going to live. "Women have often felt insane when cleaving to the truth of our experience. Our future depends on the sanity of each of us, and we have a profound stake, beyond the personal, in describing our reality as candidly and fully as we can to each other." She adds, "The possibilities that exist between two people, or among a group of people, are a kind of alchemy. They are the most interesting thing in life."

Because I could not bear to see him in tears, I agreed to stay for six months and see if we could change. But I was angry at those tears and what felt like my weakness, and in my anger I said every word I thought—how crazy I felt and how mean, the way I am never satisfied and cannot imagine a future where I ever could be. He was kind and I told him I believed his kindness to be a lie, so then he was less kind and in that way even more.

It was a slow spell and often a very boring and repetitive one, punctuated by rituals like watching him run the vacuum cleaner and fold the laundry for a change while I repeated such refrains as "I am the opposite of sorry." But in the end there was a transformation. I could see that he was not a cottar, I was not a witch, he was not a laird, I was not on fire. We were only each other. An apple tree grows in the front yard now, too young to bear fruit, but leafy and spreading her branches over the hyssop filling a bed at her feet. I look out at her in the morning while everyone is asleep and notice I am content.

I have a friend who likes to ask from time to time if I am still in love. One of my answers is: I stayed because he wasn't what I was looking for, but wasn't not what I was looking for either. Another: I never could find anywhere to put it, so I carry this floating feeling of infinite possibilities I think other people call love. Like a person with nothing to gain and nothing to lose. It has made me more dangerous and more kind than I ever would have figured out how to be on my own. A little like a bird call, sometimes lilting and sometimes squawking in the perfect quiet of my ear.

Brian spent the rest of that trip collecting hagstones and I will admit every night as he emptied his pockets of the day's discoveries, some the size of an oak leaf, others no bigger than a violet, I saw him more clearly and loved him more truly than I ever had before.

Double Vision

My daughter is tall enough now to reach the stereograph viewer I bought at an auction for fifty dollars after intense bidding that left the auctioneer laughing at the way I jumped up my number, giddy like a rookie, and bid against myself.

She lays on the couch in the bathing suit she never takes off and says things from behind that mask of carved mahogany eyes. "This waterfall gives me a papery feeling." "The Eiffel Tower gives me a papery feeling too." "This pig is sort of like nothing."

The paper feeling is a parlor trick. The glasses put the same image in front of each of your eyes, but the wooden divider down your nose keeps the optic nerves from synthesizing the two images in the usual fashion. They still become one, but in rough, shadowless perspective, as if foreground and midground have been cut loose and propped up like stage settings.

After a while this sort of looking gives you a headache. The sensation of a mind grinding itself to reconcile two distinct pieces of information into one is not unlike the twinge I sometimes get when I try to understand the absurdities of things people have said they believed. The wandering uterus, for example, a geocentric model of the universe, Blue Lives Matter. It is the kind of headache for trying to understand why our courts have ruled that we can't retroactively reverse the convictions of witches. In part, they say, because what's the point? But also, because what do we know of what those long-ago judges knew?

The philosopher Bertrand Russell explains the dilemma this way: "All our thinking consists of convenient fictions, imaginary congealings of the stream: reality flows on in spite of all our fictions, and though it can be lived, it cannot be conceived in thought."

Everything you think you have seen is actually your visual cortex conversing with the rest of your occipital lobe about their best guesses for smoothing out the many gaps in their sensory data to create a coherent image. Even if you actually saw Ursula Kemp's lamb shake off his wool and clumsy hooves, to stand up straight as a demon man named Jack, you couldn't really have seen it.

People who don't really seem to be listening have suggested I take comfort and refuge in the great sameness of our whole society of brains filling in the same sort of gaps with the same sort of logically blurred assumptions. They say we're all in this together, so don't worry about the impossibility of ever sharing in the same truth. But I have lived too much evidence to the contrary. I could only feel better if everyone was worried and admitted to being worried about the impossibility of sharing the same external reality. Then at least we could know we have worry in common.

In a complete reversal from all the stories we usually hear and I usually tell, there was once a woman who couldn't convince the villagers she was a witch to save her life. The man who wrote the account didn't preserve her name, only that she was desperate to prove to her neighbors that she could fly and consort with demons. So she got them all to watch as she covered herself in a mysterious ointment that scientist-historians today think was derived from a poisonous mushroom. She passed out and while she was unconscious the people did everything they could to wake her—they shook her and said her name and hit her. Then they hit her a lot and burned her in various places on her body. But she did not stir.

Later, when the ointment wore off she tried to tell them how she had been flying, but all they wanted to talk about were the things they had done to her while she lay there going nowhere. It took her awhile to feel the pain of their proof, but when she could fully sense herself again, she said she believed, regretfully, their version of events.

This morning at the stoplight on my walk home, a man who has been walking our town's streets with a cart full of everything he owns for the past few years was talking to me. The accounts of witches often remind me of how frightened the most secure people in our society are of the most vulnerable. Ursula Kemp, a widow who could barely keep her son fed, seemed to the warm and well-housed like the kind of person who would keep the spirits of two evil men and two evil women in pots on her stove.

As this man, who is after all one of my neighbors, was talking to me in a language I could not entirely follow, I was aloof, but not cold, and agreed with minimal but not no eye contact that yes, he was right, when the light changed we would cross the street in the same direction. And yes, that was ok with me. I was sad that he felt like he had to ask my permission to cross together and wondered what had happened to make him think such permission was necessary.

He held out his hand with a wry sort of smile and I thought we were going to handshake a seal of our mutual understanding and agreement vis-à-vis this business of crossing the street when the light changed.

I guess I was dumb to assume I knew what he would do next, but he reminded me in his nervous sway and fleeting eye contact of other people without homes I have known and orphans and high kids and hungry ones and that time I taught high school in a place where we were all just a little on edge because of how the campus was ringed with barbed wire. I thought I understood well enough the kind of moment we were having. And anyway, I crave these little moments when the external world between me and someone else becomes the same for a minute. I like to think that kindness is a kind of nerve between two identical pictures set before two different eyes.

But this man didn't shake my hand or slide his palm or press his knuckles to mine in a gesture of solidarity and understanding. He just wove his fingers through mine and held on. The red light at this intersection, I thought, must be the longest a city engineer has ever invented. Finally I pulled my hand away roughly. I hated to do it; I didn't want to be one more person afraid to touch him, but I also didn't want him to become attached. I crossed in the opposite direction of him and of where I meant to go.

I have a papery feeling today. More than most days, I have a papery feeling. This is not about the guy on the corner. It's about why I no longer have the wherewithal to stand very long with the guy on the corner. He has nothing to do with the things that have happened, I thought, but I have something to do with the things that have happened. And lately I seem more a person who needs a caseworker than the caseworker herself.

People who don't really seem to be listening have given me a pamphlet that says all of this is normal. That one in seven women have been afraid for their safety or the safety of a loved one, that one in four have been just plain afraid. Within this subgroup, 67 percent report being afraid it's never going to stop. Forty-five percent miss five or more days of work. One-third pack up their lives and try to start again somewhere far away. Statisticians have not asked how many of the women blame themselves for not having seen into the future of the mind of another person in a different reality, but anecdotally, I haven't yet met the woman who doesn't.

The external world is scary for everybody if we pay attention. That is something else we could have in common, but somehow don't. That is the part that frightens me. Also, that when I asked for help from the proper authorities, they said I was overreacting. I was trying to be careful and diplomatic about the extreme difficulty of truly interpreting another person's meanings or intentions, so I did not ask why I was the only woman in a roomful of proper authorities. I am afraid they are right and I am overreacting, I am afraid they are wrong and I am not. I am afraid that we are nothing but metaphors to each other, two eyes divided by a line we can never cross. I am afraid that sometimes one eye goes blind, and neither of us can tell if it is mine or if it is yours.

The Witch of Eye

To read the history of Margery Jourdemayne, the Witch of Eye, is to ask over and again: Did any of it happen? Did any of it happen for the reasons we think?

For years, leading up to her trial in 1441, Margery had been known as someone who could provide potions useful in advancing love, curing impotence, bringing about conception, or ending pregnancy. The wife of a cowherd, more often she was seen in the company of learned men, astrologers, and well-born ladies.

Her client, Eleanor Cobham, was wife of the successor to a very young and sickly King Henry VI. Eleanor, it seems, wanted to know if the boy would die in time for her to become queen.

For my part, I would prefer not to know the future, it being the place where I and others die sooner than I would wish. But I wouldn't object to knowing whether there really is a future waiting for us, staying up late and worried into the night watching for our little lights returning home to punctuate the darkness.

As we drive through the ancient pine forests of this sea-battered island as far from home as we can get, my daughter in a booster seat in the back, my husband with his eyes fixed on the road, I have been passing the time by reading us all fairy tales about deals with the devil.

In general it is brothers or soldiers who have three years or ten to crack the whip that summons treasures or pull out of the coat's magic pockets as much gold as they like. They know exactly how long they have to enjoy their life and they enjoy it heartily right up until that last month or year when they get clever about riddles and crafty about contracts.

When they win their souls back, they win that big expansive blue sky of a life that is now nothing but the most exquisite pleasure of undeserved extra.

I have not yet read the account of a woman making a pact with a devil that ends so well.

The only accounts we have of women doing such things are in the court documents written to justify the violence done to them.

Margery Jourdemayne was burned for treasonable witchcraft after constructing a star chart that foretold the death of the king. An act to which she confessed. She and her accomplices were also accused of, but denied, the more serious charge of trying to call up spirits from the infernal world by making an image in wax and then setting it before a fire to melt, "expecting that, as the image gradually faded away, so the constitution and life of the poor king would decay."

Bertrand Russell spends a lot of time in *Our Knowledge of the External World* thinking about what it means to use science and logical reasoning to know the future. He says, "It is necessary to shut out, by an effort, everything that differentiates the past and future. This is an extraordinarily difficult thing to do, because our mental life is so intimately bound up with the difference."

I have spent much of my time in recent months trying to see into the future of another mind. And I have been trying to see into the past of how that person sees me. I have been spending much of my time walking a very large dog bought at some expense because she is the kind of large dog that makes a person step back and take a breath. I have been wanting to go back in time and make everything different. In a daze I have accompanied my husband on tours of one house after another, because our current address, it seems, cannot be erased from the external world. I have been collecting documents for the affidavit. I have been on the phone with authorities trained to tell me they cannot speculate into the future from the collection of facts about the past in their files. I have spent much of my time in recent months learning about our responsibilities and vulnerabilities and liabilities to each other. Liabilities and vulnerabilities and responsibilities that include what I can and cannot say to you now.

According to Bertrand Russell, knowledge of the future means real knowledge of each other. "Historically, the notion of cause has been bound up with that of human volition," he says, laying out his axioms of logic through consideration of the case study he finds in Brutus's assassination of Caesar. Desire, he says, "causes a certain act because it is believed that desire will cause the person's act; or more accurately, the desire and the belief jointly cause the act." He observes that "almost our whole vocabulary is filled with the idea of activity, of things done now for the sake of their future effects."

But when the desire is for a future that cannot be made to exist? Like the one I used to think I was walking into. Even if there are infinite futures, the one you want is probably still not on the list of what's possible. Also, the number of potential outcomes narrows as you get closer to the moment that is the present. Which, depending on where you are when the walls are closing in, can be quite frightening.

Bertrand Russell is trying to be helpful to all of us who wish to be safe from each other but also gentle and good and meaningfully connected. "What happens now can only be accounted for, in many cases, by taking account of what happened at an earlier time." When we do not understand a person's past actions or their present desires, when their gait is unsteady and they twitch in a way our old instincts regard with alarm, we might respond with fear or we might respond with anger. "People who have never read any psychology seldom realize how much mental labour has gone into the construction of the one all-embracing space into which all sensible objects are supposed to fit." We might also respond with sorrow when someone cannot control their desires or their effects, and that there is nothing and never has been anything we could have done to change that.

What I don't understand is why a witch like Margery, who could see so clearly through the king's public face, didn't look at the people on the scaffold preparing to die and also think, "Why should it be you and not me?" But of course the future only seems short after the fact, it tends to be slow in coming and its dangers only obvious later. I do not think I am in danger right now. Who knows? Maybe I'm even not.

There is the one where the devil tells the father he'll make him a rich man if he gives him what's behind the barn. The father thinks it's the apple tree behind the barn, but of course it's his daughter.

> The daughter was a clever girl who drew a protective circle and kept herself inside. She was too clean for the devil to take her this way. So the devil gave her father a choice: Take away her water or die. The father took away her water, but she cried enough tears to wash herself. So the devil gave the father another choice: Cut off her hands so can't wash herself or die. She held out her hands while her father cut them off. Then she cried enough tears to wash herself clean once more, down to the bloody stumps. So the devil gave up. She too left her father's farm after that, in the opposite direction, for obvious reasons, and ended up later on married to the king.

> While the king was off to war and she was giving birth, the devil came
> back to try again. She had the baby tied to her back and set off into the
> forest. An old beggar man appeared in time to hold the baby to her breast
> so it could eat. Then he pointed her to a magic oak tree and when she
> wrapped her arms around it, her hands grew back. He showed her an
> empty cottage where she lived in simple happiness with her baby. In time
> the king found her there and they lived in joy for the rest of their lives.

My husband treads water in this blue lake ringed by mountains and
trees, while our daughter practices pushing off from the shallows to
reach him at the edge of deep. I sit on the banks watching an eagle
grab a fish from the waves lapping the far shore. We ask each other if
that was really a happy ending, or if the devil will just keep coming
back from time to time, to see if he can't catch her now. We wonder
who that old man really was. We are, of course, thinking about our
own lives, to which we must eventually return, and thinking about
what might be waiting for us when we do.

"Not only do memory and hope make a difference in our feelings
as regards past and future, but almost our whole vocabulary is
filled with ideas of activity, of things done now for the sake of their
future effects."

Unlike her servant Margery, Eleanor Cobham was highborn, so her
punishment was not execution. Instead she was paraded through
the street while a candle tied to her hand burned down into a nub
atop an agonizing wound. Then she was exiled to the Isle of Man

to spend the rest of her life looking across the water toward her old home.

Did she really want the king dead? Or did she just need someone to chart all of the possibilities for the future so she wouldn't feel so rattled with hope and fear of her own stars? These are among the endless sky of things we cannot possibly know.

The Invention of Roses

orothy, according to this and that lying storyteller of a medieval historian, was taken before a judge and tortured for the witchcraft of refusing to marry a powerful man.

And then tortured for the witchcraft of returning from the tub of boiling oil unharmed.

And subsequently for surviving unmarked for nine days in a deep prison without food or drink.

For saying she was fed on the succor of God's angels.

For being fairer and brighter to look upon than ever before.

For the descent of a multitude of angels and the sound of the demon fiends in the air wailing, "O Dorothy why dost thou destroy us and torment us so sore?" she was hanged on the gibbet and rent with hooks of iron. On and on it went, graphic and strangely erotic, as the martyrologium always are. What more proof could a judge possibly need?

To understand the actions of the judges, it is helpful to remember her crime was never that she displayed too little of her power.

Near the end of her trial, she gave a very long speech about faith in God that only a priest could love. The judge asked, "How long wilt thou drag us along with thy witchcraft?" She answered, "I am ready to suffer for my lord, my spouse, in whose gardeyne full delicious I have gaderd rosis and apples." Then she bowed her head and the man cut it off.

She bowed her head and the man cut it off, but not before she was dragged through the streets to the place of execution.

She bowed her head and the man cut it off, but not before Theophilus, a notary of Rome, mocked her from his jeering place on the side of the road by asking for roses and apples from her spouse's garden even though it was midwinter.

She bowed her head, but not before a child with star-filled eyes came to her carrying a basket with three roses and three apples. And not before she sent that boy to find Theophilus.

To convert him and save his soul and set him on his own path to glorious martyrdom, the fifteenth-century account claims. But you could also say she was trolling him. In any event, by this miracle the city of Caesarea in Cappadocia, which is in present-day Turkey, was converted and saved.

This was a reassuring story to medieval Christians who liked to tell themselves they understood what they needed to of this faraway place where their soldiers set forth on crusades even as heretics at home began to burn in ever greater numbers. In this way it reminds me very much of our war, our president, our police beating batons against their shields as they chant through body armor and face masks, "Whose streets? Our streets." It reminds me of every headline in the paper every morning of this year or that one.

For preaching of Dorothy's miracle in the streets, Theophilus was cut into small pieces and fed to the birds.

For reasons that are unclear to me, the Church has since sanctified Dorothy and Theophilus, suggesting we should take comfort in this tale.

For reasons that are unclear to me, considering she was decapitated, not burned, Dorothy was named a special protectress against fire, lightening, and thundering.

Everything is coming up roses, Sir John Mandeville said, in another fifteenth-century collection of marvelous and chiefly untrue accounts of far travels. In Bethlehem, he wrote, a woman was sentenced to burn for consorting with demons. She professed her innocence with the fervency of a Desdemona cultivar in full bloom. She prayed to the lord as if she were offering a bouquet of those award-winning Eleanors.

When she entered her pyre, the branches that had been licking flames became boughs laden red with Happy Christmas, the branches not yet ignited became boughs of blossoms as white as the Sir Galahad. "And those were the first roses and rosers that any man saw, and thus was the mayden saved through the grace of God."

By Mandeville's account, the place of this miracle became a great lake of rose bushes that stretch as far as the eye can see and many crusaders clipped huge blossoms of the damask as their horses waded through.

One of the ways I know I am entirely and really here is to walk in the fall woods among the bare and fragile trees. Witches'-broom, the common name for a deformity in a woody plant, is a disease that changes the natural structure so that a mass of shoots grows from a single point. After the leaves fall, you might see some poor tree looking over-nested or, if it is very far gone, its crown looks like a heart pincushioned by arrows. In roses the foliage becomes distorted and frazzled. The leaves become so red they are almost purple. They refuse to open any further than a tight rosette and become excessively thorny.

I have little interest in roses. They are ugly and too precious. I just like the way a dying girl flipped off an asshole and it got called a miracle. And then that asshole had a change of heart.

I like the way people could imagine themselves making a mistake and God saving them from it, though people who think God will save them from their mistakes worry me too.

The wild rose of the Teutons symbolized battle, death, the underworld. Their adolescent soldiers charged into the fight garlanded with roses. They called the battlefields where they fell rose gardens.

Rose—Hebrew for first blood spilled on the earth.

Rose—Greek for the blood of Xerxes.

Rose—Christian for Mary the Mother, for virtuous suffering and virtuous joy, for virgins devoted to God.

Rose—French for prostitute.

Rose—Roman for decadence.

Rose—English for a certain kind of power and the exchange of sweet secrets.

I have never been given roses by a man who wasn't making me uncomfortable with how hard he was, it seemed, trying to earn, or maybe even buy, me.

Rose — nineteenth-century apothecary for headache, hysteria, and other female complaints.

A popular opinion is that roses mean beauty. A popular opinion is that the pursuit of beauty will lead us to justice. Beauty means many things, of which truth and justice seem to be the most rare. Roses, of any color, are the symbol of people telling themselves what they want to hear and then giving a bouquet of it to someone else, with a note on the card that says in fine calligraphy, "Believe me when I say..."

In one tale the foam that dripped from Aphrodite as she emerged from the sea turned into white roses. The tears she shed over the body of her beloved Adonis turned them red. In another version Aphrodite, the goddess of love and beauty, emerged from the sea for no other reason than that was where Ouranos's testicles fell when his son Chronos cut them off with a sickle.

The Invention of Mothers

Set chopped up his rival Osiris and scattered the pieces across the world.

Isis was the first queen and the first witch. The first spell went like this:

> For a year Isis roamed the earth gathering up the pieces. Then she molded the one bit that could not be found out of clay. Was it his penis? His heart? His soul? It is unclear, but with this piece she made in hand, she could breathe the words that brought her beloved back to life.

Her magic only lasted a night, but that was long enough to conceive a child who would grow up to make Set pay.

———

The Gertrude bird first came into the world when a woman named Gertrude refused to feed Christ and Saint Peter. Now she is a woodpecker and makes unpleasant noises. I recognize this woodpeckered woman turned nagging bird by dissatisfied men. I recognize a version of myself and my mother and hers in such mean wizardry.

———————

Dido was the heir to her father's throne, but the people would only accept her brother. She smuggled away a fortune on their behalf, but they called her prostitute. She sailed across the sea to found a new city on a hill, but they would only accept her husband as leader. When she is called Dido her name means beloved and wanderer. In an older version of the story she is called Elisha and her name means creator god and fire and woman.

When she could take no more, she made a pyre and threw herself on it.

———————

I read the picture-book version of *Jason and the Argonauts* to my daughter on a day when she was shaken by a boy as he told her to "Shut up, Bossy." She thinks a tale of adventure will make her feel better.

Much about motherhood is a challenge, but among its comforts is how I get to read so many things I never knew before and never knew I needed. For example, I didn't know *Jason and the Argonauts* is really *The Witch Medea Gets Your Golden Fleece for You, You Fucking Incompetent*.

On the night of her escape with Jason and her father's fleece, Medea chopped up her brother and strewed the parts of him around the forest so their father would be stopped by grief and the duty to gather the pieces of his son back up.

I can't read this scene without wondering what that brother did to her, what her father did. The book says Hera cursed her to love Jason. But how many times have I read the word *seduced* when what happened was *raped*? Read *loved* but understood *imprisoned*? I think a *curse from Hera* meant *escape from an abusive situation by any means necessary*.

———————

In search of Dido's Carthage I stumbled on the story of Furra, a medieval queen of Sidama, in present-day Ethiopia. She ruled for seven years, advising the women of her kingdom never to submit to the men. Eventually the men tricked her into riding a wild steed that tore her body apart.

There is a little poem about all the places in the countryside that are named after her, Seyoum Hameso documents in *The Oromo Commentary*:

Her shoulders dropped in Qorke,

Her waist dropped in Hallo,

Her limbs dropped in Dassie,

Her genitals dropped in Saala,

Her remains dropped in Kuura.

In these places men, it is said, beat the ground in disgust. Women pour milk on the ground at the mention of her name.

———————

She is so young, this daughter of mine—does she even remember the boy in last year's grade who wouldn't stop kissing her? Elbows, the tip of her ponytail, small nuisances to make her cry with fury that she couldn't make him stop.

———————

Beyond the sea came many more adventures resolved by Medea's magic. She showed some daughters a spell whereby she turned an old ram into a young one after dropping it in her boiling cauldron. Do we believe the daughters when they say they only wanted to restore their father's youth? They swore before his boiled corpse they thought surely it would work. Personally, I think of this chapter as Medea's "Spell for a Good Cover Story Which She'll Give to Any Woman Who Asks."

It's true I pretty much never believe a white man assaulted by a woman didn't have it coming. "What did you do?" I ask such a man, as I have so often been asked. "It takes two to fight," I parrot. Maybe he should have walked away and hidden in a bathroom stall to cry like the rest of us.

When she asked the teacher to make that boy stop kissing her, the teacher said it was sweet, he had a crush. That was when I told my daughter she should push this child as hard as she could and tell him to kiss the dirt instead. But already she was too afraid.

Another of Medea's clever deeds was to feed raw meat to the Witch of the Woods and her hounds so the Argonauts could pass safely. The men ran in terror past the crone crouched and devouring, her face blood-stained with gluttony, while our sorceress lingered to say goodbye with affection to a woman we realize is her friend and sister in the craft. If any moment in this story can be made real, I want this friendship with the woman who will grow up to become Baba Yaga in her house of sweets to be the one.

Were I ever going to advise a daughter that boys will be boys, it would be in the face of what was done to Talos. Talos, a man of stone and fire, stood at the shore doing his job stopping people who should be stopped. It seems clear to me that Jason should be stopped. But Medea tricked the monster into letting her unplug the nail that held in his ichorous fire. He dies in her arms, floating in the sea, asking when she was going to fill him back up with the immortality she promised. How tenderly she cradles him as she is killing him. Then I remember he was a volcano man who wanted immortality on top of that. Typical.

There was a boy my mother encouraged me to hit. Years passed before he forced me to the edge of my own courage. It's true what the principal said to me in the office after sending him back to class, that he was smaller than the other boys and treated by them with cruelty. It is also true that when my mother was asked to pay for the glasses I broke in a bloody smear across his face she said the only part of this that made her sorry was that it had taken me so long.

She'd promised me and I think she really believed that one good fight would be enough, but I had to hit him again a year later. And then came another boy and others after that.

———

Gertrude Bell, 1868 – 1926, was an intrepid linguist, mapmaker, diplomat, and spy. She is credited as essential to the British endeavor of taking over Persia, making her the iconic embodiment of the white feminist problem. She was known as "Khatun, the Uncrowned Queen of Iraq."

What to make of her death by sleeping pill overdose?

From Bell's papers: "There is a moment, too, when one is newly arrived in the East, when one is conscious of the world shrinking at one end and growing at the other till all the perspective of life is changed."

I'm afraid sometimes I'm becoming a Medea who can't find the limits of her own vengeance. Who would destroy everything, including her own joy, to see the world made so fair a woman can commit any atrocity a Jason can. And I think of how a Khatun may prefer to hide her face in the lie that she has no power over the moral responsibility of knowing exactly how much she is capable of.

———

On the day my daughter shed those hot tears, I had been in an important meeting. There is not much about it that I can tell you. I will say only that my HR rep began by noting he thought at first I was one of the undergraduates. I was thirty-six, had a child, a PhD and four books to my name. Shall I tell you how long my skirt was or how demurely my hair pulled back? Because I checked these things before and after, as this life has taught me to do. The man chuckled like it was some kind of compliment to call a grown woman "cute" in front of the university's Threat Assessment Team and that giant binder of Title IX policies at the center of the table. The hour ended in bitterness and resentment on all sides.

———

I have these dog-eared pages with one version of the tragedy after another. I have my *Essays and Speeches* by Audre Lorde and my *Essential Essays* of Adrienne Rich. I have a dried-out highlighter. I have anger and anger to spare. And so I have decided to follow my fury off the island and across the seas through whatever current it charts. As an experiment in living with something besides fear and the sound of my own misplaced apologies.

What does a child who pushed another child deserve? Not a bloody nose and the taste of his own tears. But it seems sometimes the world only gives us everything, or nothing.

You will never get me to believe Medea killed her children and showed their corpses to cheating Jason just to make him grieve. I don't care how many times you put Euripides on a stage. I don't believe it in part because Medea isn't real so I don't have to, but also because there are many versions of the story, some recorded and some lost in the mist of a long oral tradition, each its own work of art or propaganda for whichever city-state in whatever geopolitical crisis a writer found themselves in. There were times and places when Medea's story had no end at all, just island after island. Sometimes she is powerful, sometimes angry, often happy, fighting maybe or victorious or eating a hunk of meat with her sister beside a warm fire crackling forth ephemeral constellations, a hibiscus flower in her hair like a girl, a sword at her waist like a queen. For as many nights as the children can stay awake to listen.

———

Rhiannon was a fairy queen, also wrongly accused of eating her child. She fell asleep and woke smeared in the blood and surrounded by the bones of a dog. For this she was turned into a horse. Sometimes literally, sometimes the story goes that she was punished for seven years at the gate of her castle wearing, like a horse, a bridle and bit, until her son, freed by the Horse Lord from captivity, at last returned home, where he was recognized instantly by his mother.

She is best known, though, for having brought into this world the Adar Rhiannon, those three magical birds who sing so beautifully they not only send the living to sleep but also raise the dead. When I imagine that song, it is always in the key of my grandmother, on a day when she was alive and happy, humming a little made-up tune as she holds my newborn sister in her arms.

———

Margaret Mee spent twenty-four years trying to find and then paint a moonflower, which blooms and dies in a single night.

She finally did this at age seventy-eight.

"Go home," she said to the children who worried over her. "You can leave me. I have slept with jaguars."

Translations of the Conclusions & Findings Report for Catalina Ouyang as the True Confessions of Johannes Junius

W hen Catalina Ouyang wrote to ask if, as part of her work on a visual art installation, I could create a poetic translation of the Conclusions & Findings section of the Title IX report from the 2016 investigation into her sexual assault at her undergraduate university, I was nearly finished writing a book about historical figures executed for witchcraft. Except I was stuck on one last chapter about a man named Johannes Junius.

I could have just cut his name from the list, finished the book, and never thought about him again. But it seemed so important, maybe even essential to the project.

———————

Because men were rarely, but not never, burned for witchcraft and I wanted to be accurate.

Because I wanted an easy answer at the wine box after readings when some case study out of a Solnit essay wanted to correct my "historical inaccuracies."

Because my point was not Woman, per se, but something about social control and the mythologies of justice systems.

Because I thought maybe men would buy one of my books for a change, if it didn't seem so entirely girly.

———————

I asked a translator how she translates. She said the hardest part of the work is moving the meaning from one epistemological framework into another.

How do you translate the word "panel"?

How do you translate "believes," which, to read these Conclusions & Findings, seems to be the only verb a panel can or cannot?

How do you convey what it means to call a woman who says she was raped "the complainant," as if her only function is to complain?

And what about calling the person she accuses "respondent," as if his sole responsibility is in responding?

———

I wasn't making any progress with Johannes Junius because my notes kept turning into an essay about the time a panel was convened to discuss the documents and security requests I myself once submitted under the auspices of Title IX. The time I don't want to talk about here.

The time I would like to, but feel I can't, talk about here.

The time that makes me so grateful Catalina decided to share what happened to her.

To open the file she sent—it's like she has taken the meanest words, the ones that question a woman's integrity and sanity, out of all of our heads and handed them to us on paper, where we can see them clearly for what they are.

When you are sitting before a panel your words aren't words, your words are evidence, your memories are words, your feelings are evidence of the opposite of your words, except when they are consistent with something the panel considers evidence. Your feelings are not well-spoken. If they were well-spoken they would be evidence, possibly of what you call truth and possibly of a truth of your alleged overreactions, misunderstandings, or lies.

A translator once told me that the first act of translation is to move silence into words.

So I began by trying to translate the cruel silences embedded within the lines of the Findings & Conclusions report of the panel.

We are unable to understand power, not the Respondent's, and not our own.

We are not able to admit uncertainty.

We are a panel and a panel has never been assaulted, never had an angry person throw keys across a room in the course of disagreement, a panel has never tried to leave a room a physically stronger person would not let them leave.

And yet a panel believes we know what happened.

We believe it was foreplay, because of how "Complainant's verbal expressions could be considered moaning."

We believe it was hot, because of how Complainant's "legs were open...such that Respondent's penis was able to reach her clitoris."

We do not believe these same statements could reasonably appear in a document where the findings are the opposite.

We do not believe it is relevant how her legs came to be open.

We do not wonder why the Complainant began to feel ill in the middle of "normal, consensual foreplay that the parties routinely engaged in given the frequency with which they had sex." We are distracted by frequent foreplay.

We do not believe that it is fucked up to use the word "gyrating" as a descriptor of a Complainant's actions during an experience she describes as being raped.

We believe only a Complainant has the power to misunderstand or lie and she wields that power expertly, as evidenced by how "the Panel found the Complainant to be well-spoken and verbally skilled at expressing her opinions."

———

When I reached their words "well-spoken," I wondered whether they meant they know a silver-tongued devil when they see one, or whether they were about to believe Catalina and then decided not to. Or if they only believe women have been raped if they are hysterical and crying too hard to talk about it. Or if they meant because she is Asian American they somehow imagined she wouldn't speak fluent English, as the clueless and ignorant so often do. Or if they meant she went on and on about consent and women's rights, to the point that the findings include the comment that "Complainant and Respondent both explained at length that the foundation of their relationship was based on Respondent's efforts to support, nurture, and respect her body and beliefs." I wondered if the panel imagined if they were her boyfriend they would want to do something to shut all this talk about bodies and support and respect and beliefs down too.

———

"It's the Law of the Father over there," my friend said about the Title IX office, from which I had just received an email with conclusions and findings, an email on which many of the people I worked with were cc'd. This was the best sad joke and most painfully relevant example of Lacanian analysis I ever heard. It was also the best translation of a panel's findings I would encounter, until Catalina said in her letter to me offering to send her full report provided I bear in mind: "The official account is often inaccurate and poorly representative of what I actually said / things that actually occurred because the entire Title IX process is an ineffectual, negligent, corrupt shitshow."

———

Because I realized if I wanted the world to get as big as I need it to be, I had to learn how to identify with male characters too.

But is that true? I never finished the essay because I couldn't figure out what was true anymore.

———

Johannes Junius was convicted in the Bamberg witch craze of 1626 – 1631 by a panel.

In his case, thumbscrews, leg vices, and the strappado were applied. Among other things, he confessed to succumbing to seduction by a succubus and flying to a Black Sabbath on the back of a dog. Like almost anybody being tortured, he did and said what he had to, to make it stop.

And then he did what not everybody is able to do — remember it is all a lie and use his literacy and money and influence to smuggle a letter with the truth out of his cell.

———

In the letter to his daughter Veronica, he wrote, "Here you have all of my confessions, for which I must die and they are sheer lies and made-up things, so help me God."

Almost every paragraph in the letter contains an apology. These are devastating to read. He feels so guilty about how he couldn't seem to translate his humanity into a language that his judges, from within the peculiarity of their official positions on a panel, would understand as human. He feels so guilty for having to tell his daughter that in the end he couldn't figure out how to do anything besides let himself die this way.

I know something of how irrationally guilty a person can feel for having been a victim. Of how someone might walk out of a room full of officials wondering how she had so thoroughly and painfully done all of this to herself. I do not know when I will ever be able to write about that with forthright clarity. So I translate what I know into essays about people who have been dead for hundreds of years, whose lives have become torn and water-stained pieces of parchment. The binding of folios of court records came unstitched. Many were lost altogether, burned in fires, thrown out with the garbage, flooded in basements. What is left is full of silences, enough silence to make room for mine and for most anyone else's.

———

... Maria Mueller, Margarethe Lezin, Daughter of George Haan (name lost), wife of George Haan (name lost), Anna Rinder ...

Some accounts say six hundred people were executed in Bamberg during the witch trials, some say one thousand. On the lists of names is Johannes Junius's wife, who died in the first wave of executions in 1617. She is recorded only as Wife of Johannes Junius, according to the common practice in the courts at that time.

... Wife of Johannes Junius (name lost), Elisabeth Kuetsch, Daughter of Rochus Hoffman (name lost), Wife of Rochus Hoffman (name lost), Barbara Ziegler, Elisabeth Buchlin ...

When Johannes Junius smuggled a letter to his daughter before he died, it was a translation of the confession he gave into the confession he meant. He is sorry he was not strong enough to defeat the inquisition. He is sorry he is only as vulnerable as any human is. He can barely write because of what they did to his hands in that place, and you can tell by the quavering handwriting on that old parchment in the archives that this is true.

It is a good translation. Anyone who reads it would believe him. Especially now that he is dead and we don't have to risk anything— not our own security or jobs or social capital or the disapproval of some other member of a panel on which we sit—to nod along mournfully with his words.

———

Dear Catalina,

I keep thinking of all the ways your case is so different from that of Johannes Junius. He, like all the witches, falsely accused his neighbors under pain of torture, for which he is sorry, but still, it is what he did. This is the opposite of what happened to you. The opposite of you, he did not willingly bring his story before a panel believing justice might be possible, nor did he willingly risk what any woman risks to say a crime was committed against her. He did not try to protect anyone else with his story.

I am so sorry I could not find a way to translate what your panel said into something poetic. Or even into a document that would make sense.

At first I thought I was translating this report for you. Because I have often asked trusted friends and family to translate such documents back to me. "Read this," I sometimes say to these people who love me, "and tell me if I'm crazy." They say the document is crazy, not me, and they are right and nevertheless I do not believe them.

I am sorry I could not find a way to translate what happened to you for you.

The best I can do is try to translate the panel's document back to the panel in the hopes that one day they will come to understand themselves.

My friend the translator says you must find the referents the readers of the other language can understand. If they cannot, the good advice is to leave some of the difficult referent untranslated as a signpost to the existence of a source text that is separate and distinct from the translation. What else can one do with Hindi's three different words for "you," for example? Or the way Turkish has a different verb tense for eyewitness reports as opposed to the tense used for hearsay, but also no verbs for "to have" and none for "to be."

Every language has its untranslatable words, the ones you must go outside of your homeland long enough that you ache and don't ache and ache for it again before you can finally say you understand what such words mean.

Some of these untranslatable words, the ones a person must, it seems, cross an ocean of experience to understand, apparently include: I *believe you*. And also, I *want the man who raped you to be made to feel more sorry than he can possibly imagine.*

Marie Laveau

To hear Zora Neale Hurston tell it, every Saint John's Eve, Marie Laveau appears atop the waves of Lake Pontchartrain with a huge communion candle burning on her head and another in each of her hands. "She rose from the bottom of the lake and walked to the shore on water."

There are other accounts of how she led the huge public dances of enslaved and freed people of color in Congo Square every Sunday afternoon. Many said the miracle was how she tamed a huge snake that entwined her as she slinked and stomped her body. But that is nothing compared to the combination of bribery and magic she commanded to get the soldiers to unlock the gates and permit the people to congregate in those later decades of slavery, when the city fathers passed one law after another, in mounting panic about the possibility of revolt.

It has long been the habit of tourists to make an X on the grave purported to be hers. The people who care for the grounds post signs begging the public not to deface her monument and signs threatening them with fines. Either way, they only manage to stop a few. Some of the vandals insist they feel Marie Laveau's old magic is at hand and they must try. Others don't believe in any of it and the word for them is assholes. They might be wearing those beanie hats that say "Voodoo" in a blood-dripping font or have a plastic, neon-colored chicken foot on a key ring. The commercialization of her legacy is as wrong historically as it is morally.

If you take one of those interminable carriage tours or ghost tours or plantation tours you might hear she organized the plaçage balls of the 1820s and '30s, which can be a way of calling her a madame or making a dirty laugh about what was once called miscegenation. With something closer to accuracy you might hear she was a hairdresser for the wives and mistresses of powerful men, which made her powerful in her own right, because gossip is a kind of magic and knowing how and when to keep a secret is a spell for compounding interest.

If you use a subaltern mode of historiography as Deborah G. Plant and Martha Ward have done in their studies of Laveau's life and legacy, you will discover how densely the systems of white supremacy were interwoven with laws designed to make a white person with even a prick of conscience become frightened and overwhelmed by the work of resistance. To make steadfast abolitionists into criminals. And to, one way or another, make sure all people of color lived like slaves. And then you will discover there were people whose names and methods were barely recorded who found ways to untie those knots.

For example, long-term sexual relationships between white men and women of color were common in the 1820s. And some of these men wanted to provide security for their partners and their children. Not all men, certainly. Not even most. But to think that even one white man might wish to claim his children, call them free, name them heirs to all his wealth—a machine of statutes was invented to prevent such transfer of property and manumission. As a free woman of color not-technically married to a white Frenchman for many years, Marie Laveau knew the system of this machine well. With her not-technically husband as a partner in the endeavor, they secured a home and income for her that could be passed down to their children. Ward is able to document a complicated network of property moving through hands within a circle of friends via gifts, exchanges, rentals, and bills of sale. The paperwork is confusing but reveals Marie Laveau to be an ingenious realtor at the center of a complicated extralegal housing market. She used her knowledge of these processes to help many other women in her community arrange contracts that would guarantee housing, financial support, and secure as much freedom for themselves and their resulting children as those times and Laveau's cleverness allowed. Other documents reveal she was similarly ingenious about transferring women and children this way and that until she massaged forth a paper that made them free. In other cases she adopted children to save them from being sold away or claimed them as hers after death so they could be properly buried. It is hard to say now how many children of her own she had, she offered herself as a mother so often.

By most accounts Marie Laveau was a profoundly ethical person, generous and kind, though she was called, on more than one occasion, "a notorious hag" in the newspapers. She attended Mass at St. Louis Cathedral every day, visited the imprisoned, nursed the sick during outbreaks of yellow fever with plant medicines that were far more effective than anything the doctors had to offer, and invited Choctaw women displaced once again from their land by the US government to set up camp in her own front yard.

Though she was known as a Vodou queen, she was also described as a conjure woman. Ward explains, "Conjure is the 'magical means of transforming reality.' Conjurers see and understand things most people cannot. They exist in two realities, use two kinds of consciousness—one for consensual realities and the other for the spiritual realms. Thus, a conjurer, like all mystics and visionaries, is two-headed."

To be two-headed is not the same thing as being two-faced. To be two-faced is, for example, a complicated cotillion of upper-crust manners where no one, not even the journalists at the daily paper, ever mentions the Fourth of July VP Fair you've been going to for your whole childhood is a cursory whitewash of an acronym for the Veiled Prophet, a decades-old Klan reference of a banner the two-faced person might call patriotism. A two-headed person, on the other hand, might be someone with the double-consciousness W. E. B. DuBois wrote about in The Souls of Black Folk. He explains that "the Negro is a sort of seventh son, born with a veil, and gifted with second-sight in this American world,—a world which yields him no true self-consciousness, but only lets him see himself through the revelation of the other world." He also praises such sight that aids African Americans in surviving in a white supremacist society, interpreting it also as the wisdom to convey different messages to different people at once.

When I heard Marie Laveau's story, I heard not the secret language in the dance of the snake or the rootwork, though there is an echo of so much beauty there, something for other audiences I am grateful to underhear. But for me the message of the sermon is to look to the jurisprudence of our consensual realities. I hear her saying to get smarter about the system and faster. To understand the man outside the US Post Office gathering signatures for House Bill No. 1427 to amend the Historic Preservation Act is selling another century of cheap sheet-metal Confederates marching across our parks. To know that the procedures to change the name of Robert E. Lee Elementary School can be found in the School Board By-Laws under Section F. Facilities Development, sub-section FF. Facility Names.

My formula for understanding witchcraft has been witch = accusation + fire, but no one ever burned Marie Laveau for anything. The whole city of New Orleans, they say, came to her for help or advice at some time or another. And yet she was never hauled before a court. This contradicts everything I have learned about witchcraft, about the cruelty in people afraid their power is slipping, and about the operations of nineteenth-century slaveholding societies.

Despite my cynical skepticism, the story the archives tell about the charmed work accomplished by Marie Laveau is clear. Her subterfuge in the service of social justice took the form of uncorrupted generosity. And she was loved in return by the neighbors to whom she opened her home and steady listening ear. Not long after her death Lafcadio Hearn wrote in an obituary in *The City Item* that she was "one of the kindest women who ever lived."

It feels like magic to read it and magic to tell it; yet also so very ordinary that you or I might even try our own hands at such a simple spell as this.

Sources

HAG, CRONE, CUNNING WOMAN, WITCH

Coles, William. *The Art of Simpling*. 1656. Reprint. Whitefish, MT: Kessinger Publishing, 2010.

Henderson, William. *Notes on the Folk-Lore of the Northern Counties of England and the Borders*. London: W. Satchell, Peyton, for the Folklore Society, 1879.

LISBET NYPAN

Stokker, Kathleen. *Remedies and Rituals: Folk Medicine in Norway and the New Land*. St. Paul: Minnesota Historical Society Press, 2007.

WALPURGA HAUSMÄNNIN

Monter, E. William. *European Witchcraft*. New York: John Wiley & Sons, 1969.

Stephens, Walter. *Demon Lovers: Witchcraft, Sex, and the Crisis of Belief*. Chicago: University of Chicago Press, 2003.

AGNES WATERHOUSE

Chapman, Frances E. "Coerced Internalized False Confessions and

Police Interrogations: The Power of Coercion." *Law and Psychology Review* 37, no. 1 (Spring 2013): 159–192.

Foucault, Michel. *The Hermeneutics of the Subject: Lectures at the College de France 1981–1982*. Translated by Graham Burchell. New York: Palgrave Macmillan, 2005.

Hester, Marianne. *Lewd Women and Wicked Witches: A Study of the Dynamics of Male Domination*. London: Routledge, 2014.

Kassin, Saul M. "Confession Evidence: Commonsense Myths and Misconceptions." *Criminal Justice and Behavior* 35, no. 10 (October 1, 2008): 1309–1322.

Kors, Alan Charles, and Edward Peters, eds. *Witchcraft in Europe 400–1700: A Documentary History*. 2nd ed. Philadelphia: University of Pennsylvania Press, 2000.

Najdowski, Cynthia J. "Stereotype Threat in Criminal Interrogations." *Psychology, Public Policy, and Law* 17, no. 4 (2011): 562–591.

THE INVENTION OF FIRE

Bachelard, Gaston. *The Psychoanalysis of Fire*. Translated by Alan C. M. Ross. Boston: Beacon Press, 1964.

Scarry, Elaine. *The Body in Pain: The Making and Unmaking of the World*. Oxford: Oxford University Press, 1985.

Sontag, Susan. *Regarding the Pain of Others*. New York: Picador, 2003.

Stephens, Walter. *Demon Lovers: Witchcraft, Sex, and the Crisis of Belief*. Chicago: University of Chicago Press, 2003.

Wick, Johann Jakob. *Die Wickiana* I. Edited by Wolfgang Harms and Michael Schilling. Tübingen: Max Niemeyer Verlag, 1997–2005.

TWO ELIZABETHS

Derrida, Jacques. *Psyche: Inventions of the Other*. Redwood City: Stanford
University Press, 2008.

Glanvill, Joseph. *Saducismus Triumphatus or, Full and Plain Evidence
Concerning Witches and Apparitions: in Two Parts. The First Treating of
Their Possibility. The Second of Their Real Existence*. London, 1681.

Stephens, Walter. *Demon Lovers: Witchcraft, Sex and the Crisis of Belief*.
Chicago: University of Chicago Press, 2003.

Todd, Kim. *Chrysalis: Maria Sibylla Merian and the Secrets of
Metamorphosis*. Orlando, FL: Harcourt, 2007.

TITIBA & THE INVENTION OF THE UNKNOWN

Alexander, M. Jacqui. *Pedagogies of Crossing: Meditations on Feminism,
Sexual Politics, Memory, and the Sacred*. Durham, NC: Duke
University Press, 2005.

Breslaw, Elaine G. *Tituba, Reluctant Witch of Salem: Devilish Indians and
Puritan Fantasies*. New York: New York University Press, 1996.

Certeau, Michel de. *The Writing of History*. Translated by Tom Conley.
New York: Columbia University Press, 1992.

Kotányi, Attila, and Raoul Vaneigem. "Elementary Program of
the Bureau of Unitary Urbanism." In *Situationist International
Anthology*, edited by K. Knabb, 65–67. Berkeley, CA: Bureau of
Public Secrets, 2006.

Schiff, Stacy. *The Witches: Salem, 1692*. New York: Little, Brown, 2015.

Woodward, W. Elliot. *Records of Salem Witchcraft, Copied from the Original
Documents*. Roxbury, MA: 1864. Facsimile of the first edition. New
York: Da Capo, 1969.

National Library of Sweden. "Codex Gigas." Updated June 11, 2020.
http://www.kb.se/codex-gigas/eng/.

Smith, Cassander L. "'Candy No Witch in Her Country': What One
Enslaved Woman's Testimony During the Salem Witch Trials
Can Tell Us About Early American Literature." In *Modern Black
Diaspora Studies*, edited by Cassander L. Smith, Nicholas R. Jones,
Miles P. Grier, 107–134. New York: Palgrave Macmillan, 2018.

Woodward, W. Elliot. *Records of Salem Witchcraft, Copied from the Original
Documents*. Roxbury, MA: 1864. Facsimile of the first edition. New
York: Da Capo, 1969.

HORSESHOES

Kelchner, Georgia Dunham. *Dreams in Old Norse Literature and Their
Affinities in Folklore: With an Appendix Containing the Icelandic Texts
and Translations*. Cambridge: Cambridge University Press, 2013.

Lawrence, Robert Means. *The Magic of the Horse-Shoe: with Other Folk-
Lore Notes*. Boston: Houghton Mifflin, 1898.

McDonald, S. W., and A. Thom. "The Bargarran Witchcraft Trial—A
Psychiatric Reassessment." *Scottish Medical Journal* 41, no. 5 (1996):
152–158.

Upham, Charles W. "The Confession of Ann Putnam." In *Salem
Witchcraft*, vol. 2, 510. Williamstown, MA: Corner House, 1971.

Williams, Huw. "The 'Powerful Myth' of the Paisley Curse." BBC News,
June 8, 2012. https://www.bbc.com/news/uk-scotland-glasgow
-west-18366305.

GLAS GAIBHLEANN

"No Use Crying: Milk and economic development." *The Economist*,
 March 28, 2015. https://www.economist.com/finance-and
 -economics/2015/03/28/no-use-crying.

Federici, Silvia. *Caliban and the Witch*. New York: Autonomedia, 2004.

Simpson, Jacqueline. *Icelandic Folktales and Legends*. Berkeley: University
 of California Press, 1972.

Sprenger, James, and Heinrich Kramer. *Malleus Maleficarum*. 1485.
 Reprint. Chicago: Acheron Press, 2012.

Whaley, Leigh. "The Wise-Woman as Healer: Popular Medicine,
 Witchcraft and Magic." In *Women and the Practice of Medical Care
 in Early Modern Europe, 1400–1800*, 174–195. London: Palgrave
 Macmillan, 2011.

HILDEGARD VON BINGEN

Foucault, Michel. *Lectures on the Will to Know*. Translated by G. Burchell.
 New York: Palgrave, 2013.

Strehlow, Wighard, and Gottfried Hertzka. *Hildegard of Bingen's
 Medicine*. Rochester: Bear, 1987.

Thiébaux, Marcelle, ed. and trans. *The Writings of Medieval Women: An
 Anthology*. New York: Routledge, 2012.

Von Bingen, Hildegard. *Hildegard's Healing Plants: From Her Medieval
 Classic "Physica."* Translated by Bruce W. Hozeski. Boston: Beacon
 Press, 2002.

THE ARISTOTLES THAT NEVER WERE

Aristotle, pseud., Marco Antonio Zimara, and Alexander of

Aphrodisias. *Aristotle's Book of Problems: with Other Astronomers,*
Astrologers, Physicians, and Philosophers: Wherein Is Contained Divers
Questions and Answers Touching the State of Man's Body: Together
with the Reasons of Divers Wonders in the Creation: the Generations of
Birds, Beasts, Fishes, and Insects, and Many Other Problems on the Most
Weighty Matters, by Way of Question and Answer. London, 1749.

Fissell, Mary E. "Hairy Women and Naked Truths: Gender and the
Politics of Knowledge in Aristotle's Masterpiece." *William and Mary*
Quarterly 60, no. 1 (January 2003): 43–74.

AGNES SAMPSON, THE WISE WIFE OF KEITH

Bamber, Linda. *Comic Women, Tragic Men: A Study of Gender and Genre in*
Shakespeare. Redwood City, CA: Stanford University Press, 1982.

Levack, Brian P. *The Witchcraft Sourcebook.* 2nd ed. New York:
Routledge, 2015.

Roxburghe Club. *Witchcraft pamphlet: Newes from Scotland, declaring*
the damnable life of Doctor Fian, a notable sorcerer, who was burned at
Edenbrough in Januarie last, 1591. A reprint from a London edition
probably of 1591. Edited by Sir H. Freeling. London, 1816.

THE INVENTION OF FAMILIARS

Rowland, Beryl. *Animals with Human Faces: A Guide to Animal Symbolism.*
Knoxville: University of Tennessee Press, 1973.

MARIA GONÇALVES CAJADA & THE INVENTION OF
LOVE SPELLS

Souza, Laura de Mello e. *The Devil and the Land of the Holy Cross: Witchcraft,*

Slavery, and Popular Religion in Colonial Brazil. Translated by Diane Grosklaus Whitty. Austin: University of Texas Press, 2004.

MEDUSA

Abusch, Tzvi, and Karel van der Toorn. Mesopotamian Magic: Textual, Historical, and Interpretative Perspectives. Groningen, the Netherlands: Styx Publications, 1999.

Bowers, Susan R. "Medusa and the Female Gaze." NWSA Journal 2, no. 2 (Spring 1990): 217–235.

Garber, Marjorie, and Nancy J. Vickers. The Medusa Reader. New York: Routledge, 2003.

H.D. Notes on Thought and Vision. San Francisco: City Lights Publishers, 2001.

Jolly, Karen Louise. Popular Religion in Late Saxon England: Elf Charms in Context. Chapel Hill: University of North Carolina Press, 1996.

Merleau-Ponty, Maurice. The Prose of the World. Translated by John O'Neill. Evanston: Northwestern University Press, 1973.

ANGÉLE DE LA BARTHE

Aquinas, Thomas. Summa Theologica. Cincinnati, OH: Benziger, 1947.

Lines, Malcolm E. A Number for Your Thoughts: Facts and Speculations About Numbers from Euclid to the Latest Computers. New York: Taylor & Francis Group, 1986.

Masters, Robert E. L. Eros and Evil: The Sexual Psychopathology of Witchcraft. New York: Julian Press, 1962.

Straw, Carole. Gregory the Great: Perfection in Imperfection. Berkeley: University of California Press, 1988.

Wakefield, Walter Leggett. *Heresy, Crusade and Inquisition in Southern France 1100–1250*. London: George Allen and Unwin, 1974.

Walter, Brenda S. Gardenour. *Our Old Monsters: Witches, Werewolves and Vampires from Medieval Theology to Horror Cinema*. Jefferson, NC: McFarland, 2015.

BLOODROOT

Hurston, Zora Neale. *Mules and Men*. New York: Harper Collins, 2008.

Wickkiser, Bronwen L. *Asklepios, Medicine, and the Politics of Healing in Fifth-Century Greece: Between Craft and Cult*. Baltimore: John Hopkins University Press, 2008.

THE LONG LOST FRIEND

Gettysburg Times. "Witchcraft Practiced in York County." Feb. 1, 1969.

Hohman, John George. *Pow-Wows or, Long Lost Friend: A Collection of Mysterious and Invaluable Arts and Remedies, for Man As Well As Animals*. 1820. Fascimile of first edition. Cabin John, MD: Wildside Press, 2010.

Hoyt, Ivan E. *Hex Signs: Tips, Tools, and Techniques for Learning the Craft*. Mechanicsburg, PA: Stackpole Books, 2008.

Kriebel, David W. *Powwowing Among the Pennsylvania Dutch: A Traditional Medical Practice in the Modern World*. University Park: Penn State University Press, 2007.

Mahr, August C. "A Pennsylvania Dutch 'Hexzettel.'" *Monatshefte für Deutschen Unterricht* 27, no. 6 (1935): 215–225.

Ahmad, Zaid. "In Quest of Indigenous Epistemology: Some Notes on a Fourteenth-Century Muslim Scholar, Ibn Khaldun (1332 – 1406)." In *Constructing the Pluriverse: The Geopolitics of Knowledge*, edited by Bernd Reiter, 240-258. Durham, NC: Duke University Press, 2018.

Dunbar, William. "From 'The Flyting of Dunbar and Kennedy.'" Translated by Kent Leatham. *Brooklyn Rail*, January 2014. https:// intranslation.brooklynrail.org/middle-scots/the-flyting-of -dunbar-and-kennedy/.

Harris, Carissa M. *Obscene Pedagogies: Transgressive Talk and Sexual Education in Late Medieval Britian*. Ithaca, NY: Cornell University Press, 2018.

Leland, Charles Godfrey. *Etruscan Roman Remains*. 1892. Reprint. New York: Cosimo Classics, 2007.

Orchard, Andy. *Dictionary of Norse Myth and Legend*. London: Cassell, 1997.

Rich, Adrienne. *Blood, Bread, and Poetry: Selected Prose 1979-1985*. New York: Norton, 1994.

Wilby, Emma. *The Visions of Isobel Gowdie: Magic, Witchcraft and Dark Shamanism in Seventeenth-Century Scotland*. Eastbourne, UK: Sussex Academic Press, 2010.

DOUBLE VISION

Cohn, Norman. *Europe's Inner Demons*. Chicago: University of Chicago Press, 2001.

Rosen, Barbara, ed. *Witchcraft in England, 1558 – 1618*. Revised edition. Amherst: University of Massachusetts Press, 1991.

Russell, Bertrand. *Our Knowledge of the External World as a Field for*

Scientific Method in Philosophy. Chicago: Open Court, 1914. Revised
    edition. London: George Allen and Unwin, 1926.

THE WITCH OF EYE

Freeman, Jessica. "Sorcery at Court and Manor: Margery Jourdemayne,
    the Witch of Eye next Westminster." Journal of Medieval History 30,
    no. 4 (January 2004): 343–357.

Griffiths, Ralph A. "The Trial of Eleanor Cobham: An Episode in the
    Fall of Duke Humphrey of Gloucester." Bulletin of the John Rylands
    Library 51, no. 2 (1969): 381–399.

Grimm, Jacob, and Wilhelm Grimm. The Original Folk and Fairy Tales of
    the Brothers Grimm. Translated and edited by Jack Zipes. Princeton:
    Princeton University Press, 2014.

Ralley, Robert. "Stars, Demons and the Body in Fifteenth-Century
    England." Studies in History and Philosophy of Science Part C: Studies in
    History and Philosophy of Biological and Biomedical Sciences 41, no. 2
    (2010): 109–116.

Russell, Bertrand. Our Knowledge of the External World as a Field for
    Scientific Method in Philosophy. Chicago: Open Court, 1914. Revised
    edition. London: George Allen and Unwin, 1926.

THE INVENTION OF ROSES   ·

Mandeville, Sir John. The Travels of Sir John Mandeville. Translated by C.
    W. R. D. Moseley. 1983. Reprinted with new introduction by C. W.
    R. D. Moseley. London: Penguin Classics, 2005.

Peterson, Joseph Martin. The Dorothy Legend: Its Earliest Records,
    Middle English Versions, and Influence on Massinger's Virgin Martyr,

University of Heidelberg, 1910. Reprint. Sydney: Wentworth
Press, 2019.

THE INVENTION OF MOTHERS

Bell, Gertrude. Letter to Dame Florence Bell, 29 January 1909.
Gertrude Bell Archive at Newcastle University. http://gertrudebell.
ncl.ac.uk/

Euripides. *Medea and Other Plays*. Translated by Philip Vellacott.
London: Penguin Classics, 1963.

Davies, Sioned, ed. and trans. *The Mabinogion*. Oxford: Oxford
University Press, 2007.

Hameso, Seyoum. "The Furra Legend in Sidama Traditions." *Oromo
Commentary* 7, no. 2, (1997): 16–18.

Hawthorne, Nathaniel. "The Golden Fleece." In *The Tanglewood Tales*.
Boston: Ticknor, Reed & Fields, 1853. Reprint. Warwickshire, UK:
Pook Press, 2016.

Stratton, Kimberly B., and Dayna S. Kalleres, eds. *Daughters of Hecate:
Women and Magic in the Ancient World*. Oxford: Oxford University
Press, 2014.

TRANSLATIONS OF THE CONCLUSIONS & FINDINGS
REPORT OF CATALINA OUYANG AS THE TRUE
CONFESSIONS OF JOHANNES JUNIUS

Burr, George L., ed. "The Witch Persecution at Bamberg." In *The
Witch Persecutions. Translations and Reprints from the Original Sources
of European History*, vol. 3, no. 4. Philadelphia: University of
Pennsylvania History Department, 1898–1912.

DuBois, W. E. B. *The Souls of Black Folk: Essay and Sketches*. Chicago: A. G. McClurg, 1903. Reprint. New York: Johnson Reprint Corp., 1968.

Hearn, Lafcadio. "The Death of Marie Laveau," Originally published in *City Item*, July 17, 1881. In *Inventing New Orleans: Writings of Lafcadio Hearn*, edited by S. Frederick Starr, 70–72. Jackson: University Press of Mississippi, 2001.

Plant, Deborah G. *Zora Neale Hurston: A Biography of the Spirit*. Westport, CT: Praeger, 2007.

Ward, Martha. *Voodoo Queen: The Spirited Lives of Marie Laveau*. Jackson: University Press of Mississippi, 2004.

Acknowledgments

I owe a great debt to Sarah Gorham and Kristen Miller, my editors at Sarabande Books, as well as to Brian Blair, Sun Yung Shin, and Maya Jewell Zeller, who all gave many helpful notes on these essays in draft form. Further thanks to Heidi Czerwiec, V. V. Ganeshananthan, Rivka Galchen, Angela Hume, Douglas Kearney, Hyejung Kook, Kate Lebo, Polina Malikin, Jenny Molberg, Sarah Nguyen, Sharma Shields, Paul Sturtz, Corinne Teed, Kim Todd, and Holly Vanderhaar for great conversations about and insights into witches and witch trials.

This book is dedicated to my mother, M. Patricia Weber Nuernberger and my sister, Sam Nuernberger, but it is also for my daughter Alice Nuernberger Blair and my grandmothers, Alice Margaret Hornung Nuernberger and Mary Margaret Keyhoe Weber. In memory of Susanne Hornung, sister to Margaret, daughter of Estelle Swederske Hornung, daughter of Maria Hagedorn Wing; Paulina Mink Hornung, sister of Tanta Lena Mink and Josephine Mink; Winifred Plowman Keyhoe, daughter of Mary Murphy Keyhoe, daughter of Bridget McDonald Murphy; Eleanora Higgins Weber, daughter of Anna Maria Janssen Higgins, daughter of Bridget McGowan Higgins. My love for Oliver

Nuernberger, Peter Nuernberger, Ken Nuernberger, George Nuernberger, Ernie Weber, and Bill Hornung is here too.

The Institute for Advanced Study at University of Minnesota provided a fellowship that helped make this work possible. I am grateful to my research assistants, Isabella Gold and Matthew Noteboom, for their help fact-checking this book, and to the DFRACS program at University of Minnesota for funding their work.

Thanks also to the journals who first published these essays in their earlier forms.

"Lisbet Nypan"—*The Collagist*

"Walpurga Hausmännin"—DIAGRAM

"Agnes Waterhouse"—*Waxwing*

"The Invention of Fire"—*Plume*

"Two Elizabeths"—*Paris Review*

"Titiba & the Invention of the Unknown"—*Public Domain Review*

"Horseshoes"—*New Territory*

"Hildegard von Bingen"—*Hayden's Ferry Review*

"The Aristotles that Never Were"—*Cincinnati Review*

"Agnes Sampson, the Wise Wife of Keith"—*Bat City Review*

"The Invention of Familiars"—*Brevity*

"Maria Gonçalves Cajada & the Invention of Love Spells"—
    Southern Review

"Medusa"—*Guernica*

"Angéle de la Barthe"—*Meridian*

"Bloodroot"— *Entropy*

"The Long Lost Friend"— *Copper Nickel*

"The Eye of the Hagstone"— *Salamander*

"Double Vision"— *The Pinch*

"The Witch of Eye"— *Florida Review*

"The Invention of Roses"— *Cleaver*

"The Invention of Mothers" — *Gulf Coast*

"Marie Laveau"— *Zone 3*

"Translations of the Conclusions & Findings Report for Catalina
Ouyang as the True Confessions of Johannes Junius" first appeared
as a hornbook in *Conclusions & Findings*, a visual art installation by
Catalina Ouyang at the NARS Foundation.

KATHRYN NUERNBERGER is the author of the poetry collections *Rue*, *The End of Pink*, and *Rag & Bone*. She has also written the essay collection *Brief Interviews with the Romantic Past*. Her awards include the James Laughlin Award from the Academy of American Poets, a National Endowment for the Arts fellowship, and notable essays in the Best American series. She teaches in the MFA in Creative Writing program at University of Minnesota.

SARABANDE BOOKS is a nonprofit literary press located in Louisville, KY. Founded in 1994 to champion poetry, short fiction, and essay, we are committed to creating lasting editions that honor exceptional writing. For more information, please visit sarabandebooks.org.